A World Citizen In the Holy Land©

I0086845

by

Garry Davis

Published by
The World Government House
POB 9390
South Burlington, VT 05407
ISBN 0-9706483-4-0

Sergeant Parsival of the Sovereign Order of World Guards raising the World Flag at "Chaggara," Hesinque, France, during the May 22, 1976 ceremony when I declared the land "world territory."

To
Bud

A Note to the Reader

The very fate of humanity is embroiled in the events in the Middle East. What is the key to solving this seemingly intractable dispute?

Because this question is so crucial for all of us, I've decided to republish this little volume first printed privately in a strictly limited unpublicized edition

It is just one man's story, but it gives new voice to the teachings of the ancient biblical prophets—one world and one human family. Though the events occurred in 1976, its theme is relevant to the ongoing conflicts and dissensions dominating today's headlines.

Abraham, the Patriarch, was the one historical figure who united both Arabs and Jews as members of one family within the larger human family.

In our monthly newspaper, *World Citizen News,* we published in 1978 an article called *The Abraham Federation,* which contained innovative ideas for generating a Mid-East regional peace strategy. The article was updated and republished in American-Arab Affairs (now Middle East Policy) in the Spring of 1991, then in *Curing World Poverty: The New Role of Property,* and finally in *Social Justice Review* in collaboration with the Center for Economic and Social Justice in 1994.

Why is it that Arabs and Jews live together in peace within in the United States and other countries? It's not because they have eliminated their disagreements or hatreds, but because they dwell under a system of law. They have raised their sovereignty to the national level. Within that system of law, there are plenty of disputes, but there are no "enemies". Enemy is by definition the outsiders. If we raise our sovereignty to the world level, if we identify ourselves as humanity, then there are no enemies.

There will still be plenty of disputes, but we'll have a system of handling them, fighting it out in courts, not on the battlefield.

Thus my theme herein is immediately relative to today's conflicts in the "Holy Land."

In that context, you, the reader and I, must now imitate the roles of the prophets themselves if we would justify both their teachings and our own earthly existence.

This, in brief, is why I am republishing this book today.

Garry Davis

Independence is my happiness and I view things as they are, without regard to place or person; my country is the world; my religion is to do good and all men are my brothers.

—THOMAS PAINE: The Rights of Man—

Universal Declaration of Human Rights

Article 1.

All human beings are born free and equal in dignity
and rights. They are endowed with reason and conscience
and should act towards one another in a spirit of brotherhood.

Article 13.

(1) Everyone has the right to freedom of movement
and residence within the borders of each state.
(2) Everyone has the right to leave any country,
including his own, and to return to his country.

Article 21.

(3) The will of the people shall be the basis of the authority of government...

Article 28.

Everyone is entitled to a social and international order in which
the rights and freedoms set forth in this Declaration can be fully realized.

Foreword

One day this winter, as I sat idly in my tiny office above Church Street in Burlington, Vermont, my eyes went past my brother Bud's picture on top of the computer monitor to the top shelf on the opposite wall. It was lined with dozens of three-ring binders embracing personal papers; newspaper clips from 1948; correspondence with heads-of-state and US presidents; the INS; the State Dept.; council members, plus myriad organizations; yearly personal correspondence; Navion files and documentation.

There, on that top shelf, was a large folder with some forgotten chapters in my life. On impulse, I pulled it down and started reading. This booklet is the result.

My visit to the Holy Land had been delayed by over 40 years. When the UN ambassador to Israel, Count Bernadette, was assassinated in 1948, the writer Meyer Levin implored me to go to Israel to replant the seed of world citizenship in that sacred land. I say "replant" because for me all the prophets from time immemorial who lived there were world citizens unfettered by divisions. Their inspired words ring through the corridors of history to our present time challenging and exposing all relativist thoughts. But the first two years of the world citizenship movement* in Europe depleted me physically and morally and I returned to my birthplace to recuperate and meditate on those historic events.

As I studied the manuscript, I thought that now, in this 50th anniversary year of the launching of the UN's Declaration of Human Rights, is the time to republish this tale, especially in view of the so-called Middle East "crisis" where violence allied with politics threatens the world community. After all, nuclear weaponry is still a national trigger-finger away from annihilating humanity itself.

The events told here followed my proclamation of "world territory," May 22, 1976, for "Chaggara," the family Alsatian home near Basel, complete with flag and "Sergeant" Parsival – a Swiss conscientious objector who did his time for years in a Swiss goal—of the Sovereign Order of World Guards.

French police milled around the local crowd, sprinkled with journalists from Geneva, trying to find a reason to arrest me (again) but left perplexed that somehow no French laws had actually been broken.

The idea of "mondialization" (declaring cities, states, etc. "global") lent itself naturally to all holy sites—temples, churches, synagogues, mosques, shrines, or whatever—being considered God's earthly "territory," that is, under the sovereign protection of world law.

That is the dominant theme herein.

While the booklet stands on its own, it is only a small piece of the mosaic that makes up one man's solo adventure in these turbulent times. But for me, it is a vital piece. I hope you may find a corresponding echo here in your own life.

If, on a larger scale, it can help influence minds and hearts in that part of our planet deemed "sacred" because of the eternal truths enunciated there, thus revealing a happier world, it may indeed nurture a greater and common good.

Then my brother Bud's tragic fate on the USS Buck at the battle of Salerno, like other "honored dead," would at last be vindicated.

—Garry Davis, Burlington, Vermont, March 15, 1988

* See *My Country is the World*

A WORLD CITIZEN IN THE HOLY LAND

Garry Davis

"Thus saith the Lord, Keep ye judgment and do justice; for my salvation is near to come, and my righteousness to be revealed." Isaiah 56:1

Take-off

The French control officer at General de Gaulle airport stared at my World Service Authority passport, thumbing through the pages rapidly. Pan Am flight 112, on which I was booked, left for Ben-Gurion airport, Israel, in just twenty minutes. It was June 12, 1976, the declaration of Chaggara as "world territory" 21 days behind me.

"You are going to Israel? But you have no visa," the young officer sitting in the elevated desk before me said brusquely,

"Oh, but I don't need a visa for Israel. I'm stateless," I said, smiling.

"One moment, please," he said, getting up. He went through a door behind him. Five minutes passed. I thought I had better hurry things up. My luggage was already on the plane. The Pan Am girl who had checked me in ten minutes before had glanced perfunctorily at the passport.

"I haven't seen one of these before," she said, surprised. "International," I returned pleasantly. "Oh, right." She tore off the ticket and handed the stub back. "Have a nice trip." I moved around the empty desk and through the door leading to the inner corridor where people were moving hurriedly in both directions. Small elegant shops lined the sides offering last-minute tax-free purchases. I looked for the airport police office.

It was directly on my left. I walked hurriedly into the office.

"Excuse me," I said to the policeman sitting at the desk, "my plane leaves in ten minutes and..."

The officer with my passport came out of the inner office. Before he could accuse me of breaking through a national frontier without authorization, I said angrily, "See here, I certainly have the right to leave France. May I have my passport, please?"

"But you have no visa for Israel. They will not let you in," he said taken aback by my attack.

"But that is, after all, my problem, not that of the French Police. Besides you are wrong. There is no need for a visa for Israel with this passport. But if you wish, we will ask the Pan Am agent to check the book."

I held out my hand. Having no immediate response, he handed back the passport. We went to the Pan Am desk in front of the corridor leading to the transit lounge.

"Do you have a book on passport restrictions?" I asked her.

She looked up from her seating board. "Why yes," she replied.

"Look, I'm on Flight 112 for Tel Aviv and the French control is concerned about the validity of my passport for Israel. Would you be so kind as to see if there are any restrictions on a WSA passport."

"Yes, certainly," she replied retrieving a thick red book from under the counter. She thumbed through quickly to "Israel," reading through the list of passport restrictions. "No, there is nothing here," she said.

I turned to the police officer. "You see," I said, "no problem." Smiling I handed the girl my ticket stub. The Police officer walked away slowly, a puzzled frown on his face. I walked swiftly to the waiting plane.

Winging across the Mediterranean, after passing over Switzerland, Italy, part of the Adriatic and the tip of Greece, I came to certain conclusions about this particular trip. Ever since the declaration of "world territory" on May 15th of "Chaggara," our home in Alsace, and Toma Sik's insistence that I come to Israel to "mondialize something in this holy land, maybe a kibbutzim," I felt that, at last, I was about to fulfill a 28-year-old promise to Meyer Levin, the writer, world citizen and citizen of Israel. We had discussed long into many nights the meaning of Israel's founding in those frenetic days of 1948 when the world citizenship movement began in Paris where Meyer lived with his vivacious wife, Tereska, also a writer. "The Jews are world citizens already," he would argue. "We've been wandering for two thousand years all over the world. Now we have our own state. It's got to be a world state or we'll make the same mistakes as everyone else."

"But a 'world state' is a contradiction in terms," I would reply. "A state is exclusive, and the world is inclusive. I agree that Jews are world citizens especially as the first people who accepted monotheism. They also understand perhaps more than most what human rights mean, having suffered their lack for so many years. However, if I came to Israel, what can I say: 'Give up your sovereignty? Declare a world government?' I would be locked up in the nearest jail and the key thrown away. Or deported on the next plane."

"Listen," he replied, "there are plenty of people in Israel who are troubled by the establishment of a new state and I don't only speak of the Hasidic Jews. A sovereign state is no permanent solution to our security. That is obvious. Come down at least and plant some seeds. Who knows what will grow?"

Zion

In the intervening years, as I read of the troubles and wars in the so-called Middle East, I remembered Meyer's words. He called himself a world citizen "Zionist!" But then what did "Zion" really mean? Was there an esoteric meaning as well as a literal one? Deriving from the Hebrew word "Tsiyon," it was originally the same as a stronghold in Jerusalem. Therefore, from "a hill in Jerusalem, site of the royal palace of David and his successors, the place of the temple, the centre of Hebrew government, worship and national life, the meaning broadens to a) The Israelites, b) the theocracy, or a church directly administered by God, or c) "the heavenly city of God."[1] Surely here was a universal connotation of the word popularly used to justify a new exclusivity, a new nationalism.

Even the prayers on Rosh Hashanah, the Jewish New Year, claiming God's sovereignty over all the earth and all humankind, imply the universality of the word:

"For the sovereignty is the Lord's, and He is the Ruler over all nations."
"In Thy great goodness be merciful unto us, unto Zion, Thy City and thine inheritance."

"The Lord shall reign forever; thy God, O Zion, shall be sovereign unto all generations."
"And Thou, O Lord, wilt rule, Thou alone, over all thy works on Mount Zion, the dwelling place of Thy glory."

Here is no narrow secularism, no frontier philosophy. Here a "Zionist," who worships the One God, Who is sovereign over all the earth and all humans, is per se, politically, a world citizen first and a national citizen second. In the 20th century, political exclusivity was no longer possible. The "Middle East" was part of the total world community. However, in the world of nation-states, it was the fuse to the world powder keg.

That was surely not what God intended as a "heavenly city."

An immense historical/political/religious drama was being enacted in "The Promised Land" with repercussions for the entire human race. When nuclear war threatened the entire territory, no one people could "own" any part of the world's surface. Absolute ownership of land was a no-win proposition.[2]

If it was indeed security the Jews sought above all, it could surely not be found behind national "defense" lines, proven hideously false since time immemorial. Indeed, the exclusivity of the state was continually denied by the Universality and the Unity of God Himself, the advocacy of which the Hebrews never relinquished, despite their monstrous suffering, but contrarily revealed in virtually every Hebrew prayer:

"Praised be Thou, O Lord, our God, Ruler of the Universe, who with Thy word bringest on the evening twilight, and with Thy wisdom openest the gates of heaven."[3]
"Hear, O Israel: the Lord our God, the Lord is One."[4]
"Lord of the world, the King supreme, Ere aught was formed, He reigned alone. When by His will all things were wrought, Then was His sovereign name made known."[5]
"And the Lord shall be King over all the earth. On that day, the Lord shall be One, and His name One."[6]

Of course I had found the same universality and unity in Christian and Moslem theology as well as Hindu, Buddhist, Taoist and Baha'i. If God was known as Yahweh, the Self, Allah, Jesus Christ, The Tao, the Absolute, Truth, Brahmin, or whatever, the universality and unity were the same. If the "Promised Land" could be equated with "the heavenly city of God," then in earthly terms, the "Promised Land" is God's global "kingdom," promised to us, the human race, by the ancient prophets.

That the Hebrews occupied a unique and rightful place in the establishment of this earthly "Promised Land" through their infusion into society of a new universal morality based on monotheism was undeniable. But this morality was more in keeping with the 20th century scientific world view than with bygone centuries of superstition, mysticism for the few, and a largely peasant agricultural life for the people.

This "vertical" view of Zion is not in contradiction to the establishment of a "homeland" for the Jews on condition they recognize at the same time their fundamental world citizenship and Homeland of the planetary community with which they are already familiar, as primordial.

World Arrival

The blue Mediterranean below me was by now a familiar sight. My first trip to India to study the Advaita Vedanta[7] with Nataraja Guru ten years before, then my rubber-boat exit from France to Italy in 1958,[8] a sales trip as overseas agent for Harris Brushes in England in 1962 to Malta, Cyprus, Greece, and Lebanon, and a second trip to India in 1973 to attend the World Conference for Peace Through Unitive Understanding in Ramanthali, all were united by this watery crossroads of the world.

As the great plane was making landfall around 8:30 p.m., I took out my passport with the embarkation card filled out and tucked inside. For "nationality," I had written "World Citizen." Let it be a test, I told myself. If Israel were a mere state among states, with no special distinction, I might be refused entry since I was identified only with a world passport. It would be ironic, I thought, but highly significant. If, on the other hand, Israel were unique in that it was composed largely of immigrants, many of whom surely lacked "proper" documentation on arrival, especially in the early days, than a committed world citizen identified as such, coming in the name of world peace, would surely be admitted.

I had deliberately not alerted Meyer Levin, Abie Nathan or any other friends of my arrival. Only Toma had been advised and then only the day before so that there would be no time to try to influence anyone in the government. Just before leaving Paris for the airport, however, I had telephoned the news desks of UPI, AFP, and AP, giving them my flight number and time of arrival. In such a situation, as usual, the media were my only "ambassadors."

The others passengers disembarked before me. Being last in line, I had discovered over the years, allowed more time for interesting debate. We crossed over the short, concrete parking space to the yawning, barnlike, brightly-lit terminal building. Airport police were everywhere. Security was tight. I remembered how Israeli agents, not French police, had individually inspected our luggage at the De Gaulle airport. Pens were unscrewed, tape recorders made to operate, bottles sniffed.

Lines were forming at the counters for passport control. Finally, I presented my passport to the young girl at the far-left counter, furthest from the police at the right.

She paged through it looking for the visa. Not finding it, she turned back to the cover. Then she looked at me sharply.

"What is this passport? And where is your visa?"

"It's what it says it is, a World Service Authority passport, issued from Basel. It's based on article 13, section 2 of the Universal Declaration of Human Rights. It says so, starting on page 37 in seven languages. Will you stamp it please? I have friends waiting."

"Not so fast," she replied, taking the embarkation card. She read it, then looked at me slowly. "I see. Please come with me."

An elderly-looking official in a gray, short-sleeved shirt, with two stars on his shoulder looked at the passport in consternation, then disgust.

"We do not recognize this passport," he said in a heavily Slavic-accented voice. "You will be on the next plane back to Paris."

"You mean Israel does not recognize a passport on the right of freedom to travel?"

"You must have a valid national passport to enter Israel," he replied brusquely as if reading from a manual.

"Has everyone who has come to Israel possessed a valid national passport?" I asked him mildly .

"I am not a historian," he replied curtly, "just a police officer. And I have my orders." He handed me back my passport. "Now if you will just sit over there," he said, indicating a bench near the control booths, "I have work to do."

So, the "Promised Land" was out of bounds for a world citizen! At least, the latest political manifestation of it. Bureaucracy moves fast, I thought, moving to the bench. The drama was an old one for me though the setting was new and perhaps the most symbolic of all. The image of "no place at the Inn" was strong in my mind as I watched the airport activity through half-closed eyes.

The modern state was the latter-day "Inn" where there is no real refuge. I thought to myself, how many are being excluded throughout the world even now? How many are waiting in airports, detention camps, prisons, or wandering city streets, living like stray dogs, also "excluded" for not having "valid" national papers?

The issue of Palestinians in Israel vividly exposed the terrible illusion of "ownership" by a state of a given piece of world territory. That, in a general sense, the planet earth "belongs" to all its inhabitants, is self-evident, admitting of no doubt. Possession of a part of it by a particular group of humans can only be considered relatively. The state, however, in making an absolute claim over a partial territory in the sacred name of "security" at once affirms that relativism thereby negating real security. Is not this illusion of absolute ownership, I thought, the seed of its own destruction, fulfilling the ancient maxim of absolute power corrupting absolutely? Moreover, is not this true of all states?

While I wondered where Toma was, a man with a camera approached. "Are you Garry Davis?" he asked pulling out an AP press card. Again I marveled at the contradiction of our global communication network and the archaic political frontier system. Associated Press and its sister wire services operated pragmatically on the basis of no frontiers in one world.

When I informed him I was, he took pictures, oblivious to the hard stares of the control officer in his little cubbyhole office.

"Why do you want to come to Israel, Mr. Davis?" he asked, pencil and pad in hand. "Are you a Jew who wants to emigrate?"

"According to the Talmud," I replied, "I'm not a Jew since my mother was not Jewish. My father was. But frankly, I don't know what a Jew is. Apparently there is a big debate about that very subject here in Israel.[9] But no, I am not immigrating. I'm a simple visitor for the first time to the Holy Land. I come in peace. I have many friends here. But it does not seem I will be admitted. I don't have what your government considers a valid national passport."

"Ha! That's good. Neither did I when I came in. But tell me, what can a world citizen do in Israel? There is a rumor that you want to declare Jerusalem an international city."

I laughed. "No, that's not true. Jerusalem is already a world city in a very real sense. And like all cities, it is in danger of nuclear destruction. That is the lesson of Hiroshima and Nagasaki. But I want only to visit the holy sites. And of course to see old friends."

"Garry, oh Garry!" a bright voice called out over the hubbub of airport noise. I looked up. Tereska Levin ran up to me and gave me a big hug.

"Why didn't you let us know you were coming? Toma is outside. He couldn't get in. It came over the radio that you were here. We could have prepared your entry. But like this, the government was caught unawares." The words came tumbling out. Tereska was as vibrant and lovely as I had known her in Paris 28 years before.

She turned to the journalist. "But it is a scandal! The Israeli government doesn't let Garry Davis in! It is a shame on all of us. Garry, what can we do to help?"

"There's the man to talk to," I replied indicating the officer. She went to his cubbyhole office. The AP correspondent and I followed.

"Do you know who this is?" she asked angrily. "He is the world citizen. I vouch for him. My husband, Meyer Levin, will vouch for him. He wants only world peace. Why can't he enter Israel. It is a scandal!"

The officer put down his pen and looked up wearily. "We do not recognize his passport. It is not valid. We know all about it. A terrorist tried to use one some months ago. He issues them to the enemies of Israel."

Now we're getting somewhere, I thought to myself. I suspected there was something more than simply not possessing a valid national passport. Tereska appeared confused. The introduction of the word "terrorist" and the charged phrase "enemies of Israel" for the moment left her speechless.

The "attack" was later reported by an Israeli government source. The source was not quoted. The so-called terrorist was not named. Again the principle of freedom of travel and restrictions in the name of state security were inter-twined to mislead the public. To mix the former with the alleged actions of an individual engaged in violent activity was to confuse human rights with penal offenses. The post office clerk who sells stamps is not responsible for the contents of the letter or package, be it a present to a loved one or a bomb. Every hardware store or drugstore sells goods which can kill, maim or otherwise violate normal civilized behavior. On the contrary, the responsibility of the individual is always engaged in conformity with existing laws.

"Anyone trying to use a world passport," I said as much to Tereska as to the officer, "with terrorism in mind is either a fool or wants to get caught. You cannot escape attention with it. With all respect, I seriously doubt any would-be terrorist would apply for a WSA passport. And also, knowing the security, both internal and external, you chaps have, whether they possessed our passport or a national passport, wouldn't matter in terms of control."

Tereska left to call Meyer who was waiting for news. The AP man left to file his story. As there were no Pan Am planes for Paris until the morning, I was confined to a cell at the airport for the night.

The "Law" of Space

The next morning at 6:00 am, I was taken in a police van to the parking space in the international side of the airport.

"I would like to see the Pan Am field manager," I told the immigration officer who opened the back door of the van.

"Why?" he asked suspiciously.

"Well, you're about to transfer me to a private carrier," I replied, "I think I have the right to speak to a representative of that carrier so that he knows my position. After all, there are no Israeli police aboard a Pan Am plane."

He gave me a quizzical look, turned and beckoned to a man standing nearby. "He is the Pan Am manager here," he said as the man approached.

"Good morning," I said pleasantly. "My name is Garry Davis, and I understand that your company has agreed to take me aboard the next flight to Paris."

"That's right," he said cautiously.

"In that case I would like to speak to the Captain of the plane."

"The captain is busy. He has no time to see you."

"Well, since he is responsible for the plane and all the passengers once the plane leaves the ground, I think he might be interested in knowing what my intentions are once we are in neutral space."

His look of surprise was reassuring. The last thing he wanted was trouble in mid-flight. And there was no law on transatlantic carriers except for the pilot flying the plane. In short, anarchy reigns between states. Therefore, carriers transferring humans between states become subject to whatever actions the passengers decided to take. Hence, the strict airport control over weaponry. Hijacking has become a terrorist's tool-in-trade.

"What do you intend to do?" he asked, eyeing me warily.

"That's what I want to speak to the captain about," I replied. "There's not too much time. Is he around?"

The captain was tall, mid-forties, with a small, well-trimmed mustache and obviously didn't want to talk with me from the cautious way he approached the van. I figured I had better put him at ease at once.

"Hi, captain. I flew B-17's during the war. 8th Air Force based in UK." He relaxed slightly.

"Mr. Bronstein says you got something to say to me."

"Yes, You probably know the Israeli police were putting me aboard your plane."

"Yeah. That's what they told me."

"Well, what they didn't tell you was that I refuse to go willingly."

"I didn't suppose you did."

"Well, as an unwilling passenger, I refuse to be responsible for my actions while aboard."

"Just what does that mean?"

"It means that you, as the captain of the plane, are colluding with what I consider an unjust action by the Israeli police. That makes you an accessory after the fact, in other words, an accomplice."

"Just what the hell do you intend to do about it?"

"Well, for starters, since I'm not a paying passenger, I will announce that fact to my fellow passengers and explain the situation."

"Forget it, Davis. You're not flying on my plane."

"Thanks, captain, I thought you'd see it my way."

I "Pass" the Flag

The frustrated police returned me to my cell. Two more Pan Am planes left that morning without me. Abie Nathan, former El Al pilot and foremost Israel peacenik, arrived that afternoon with a reporter from Ma'ariv. He was on the 19th day of a 40-day fast for peace. His "Peace Ship" was still anchored 3 miles and several feet out in the Mediterranean sending out rock music and peace messages.

"You've won, Garry," he told me matter-of-factly. "They know they can't deport you. However, they're not going to release you from here. Moreover, the longer you stay, the more embarrassed the government will be. Also your friends. I'm not saying this is good or bad. But the decision is now up to you."

"But why won't they let me in?" I asked. "Surely they're not afraid of me?"

"Oh no, it's not you personally," he replied. "You have many friends in the Knesset. It's the passport. They're afraid of the precedent. And that story about the terrorist who tried to use a

7

WSA passport, whether true or not, was put out by a minister, so the government has taken an official position. They can't back down now."

"Amazing. The only passport which represents the very right that the Israeli government uses against the Soviet Union to allow Soviet Jews to emigrate is condemned here in Israel."

"But why didn't you let us know you were coming?" he asked. "We could have prepared the way."

"I didn't want the way prepared, Abie," I replied smiling. "This way, the issue is clear-cut. Israel is a nation-state like all the others. It does not consider the person, only his papers. The major difference here is that this is the land of the prophets. I can't help but wonder what they would have thought of your government's decision."

He laughed, delighted with the thought. A man 19 days into a 40-day fast attains a highly translucent perception of righteousness often hidden by the press of daily necessities.

"Good point," he said. "I daresay had you been around then, you would have issued them all world passports."

"Why not?" I returned. "For me, they were all world citizens. But seriously, Abie, I have no intention of remaining in this cell for the rest of my life. Besides, I'm due in Washington on July 4th for the Bicentennial Celebration. So, here is what I would like to do. I will issue you a world passport, here and now. It will be as sort of transfer of mission. Then you go into Israel with the same passport the government refused to accept for me. Then I agree to leave. What do you say?"

"Of course. Gladly. I am honored," he replied.

I opened my traveling World Government Issuing "Office," took out a blank passport, a fiscal stamp, the WSA dry seal, a Polaroid camera, the riveting machine and a WSA rubber stamp which would cover my signature and the fiscal stamp. The Ma'ariv journalist was highly amused, his notebook filling rapidly.

"In the name of human rights and fundamental freedoms, world law and its sovereign institutions, I hereby present you, Abie Nathan, world citizen, citizen of Israel and devoted worker for world peace, with this honorary world passport symbolizing the oneness of humankind and of our true world which the ancient prophets who walked this holy land exemplified and taught."

He took it with both hands delighted, checked his passport picture, gave me a hug while the reporter closed his notebook with a "Mazel Tov!"

The airport officials were delighted with my decision, releasing me immediately from the cell and installing me in a small dormitory on another floor of the same building.

"Would you like to take a tour of Tel Aviv tonight?" the captain asked me incongruously after Abie had left. Your plane leaves tomorrow morning. You will be our guest."

"But I have still have no papers you recognize," I reminded him.

"Oh, that does not matter now," he replied, smiling. "We accept your promise that you will leave tomorrow. We know you are a man of your word. Besides, one of my security team will accompany you."

"Fine, I accept with appreciation. And can we stop at Mr. Nathan's apartment as he mentioned taping an interview for his show tomorrow?"

"Of course," he said. "No problem."

On the drive into Tel Aviv in the small army truck that evening, the young sergeant was talkative.

"I was born here, in '48, in the middle of all the confusion. My parents came from Bremerhaven originally. They survived Auschwitz. They won't talk about it even now. There are many here like that."

"Tell me," I asked, "Are you a Zionist?"

"Zionist! Me? Of course not. Why should I be a Zionist? I am an Israeli citizen. That is enough."

"But do you go to a synagogue? I mean, are you religious?"

He seemed more reluctant at this question. "Well, as a soldier, there is not so much free time. I use it to be with my family. Oh, we celebrate the High Holidays like everyone else, but all this religious business, I don't go for it myself. I mean, it's all right for those who like it like the Orthodox Jews, but I'm more into politics, like you."

Not quite like me, I thought grimly.

The streets of Tel Aviv were alive with people. Occasionally, I saw elderly couples with guns over their shoulders.

"They're part of internal security," the sergeant told me proudly. We arrived at Abie's small but luxurious apartment in a modern building looking out on the dark Mediterranean. He greeted me warmly and we did a half-hour taped interview for the next day's transmission. My voice was allowed into Israel, and my ideas, but not my body.

I had a through ticket to New York but no visa for the USA. It proved a costly mistake, however, to have booked a flight through Paris and not Rome. My luggage carried 150 Leather-bound WSA passports, a gift from a West German world citizen bookbinder, plus 200 standard passports and much documentation, all destined for the Washington DC WSA office. I did not think there would be a passport control at General De Gaulle airport, especially since I would remain in transit. But I did not count on the craftiness of either the Pan Am manager at Tel Aviv who apparently informed the French control police by telex that I possessed no US visa, nor of the French police themselves who, after interrogating me, proceeded to confiscate not only all the blank passports but also the one I carried as a personal travel document on which my Washington, DC address was inscribed.

I was furious at my own stupidity for having fallen once more into the hands of the French police. Controlling my anger, I said to the control officer, "Since you have taken all my papers, how do expect me to re-enter France?" Our treasury could ill afford the replacement of the precious documents. Now I would have to return to St. Louis to replenish my stock as well as to obtain a new passport for myself.

"You will not re-enter France," he replied haughtily. "When you are refused entry from another county, it is as if you did not leave France. You tricked us when you left. It will not happen again."

So ended my first aborted attempt to enter the Holy Land.

Second Take-off

"But you don't need a visa with this document."

The young, pretty, dark-haired girl at the visa desk of the Israeli Embassy in London handed me back my stateless document. It was now January 10, 1977. The door to France had again slammed shut behind me.[10] Once again, as in 1948, I was forced to "hit the road," the "legal" frontiers of both Switzerland and France closed to me. My destiny, I was now convinced, lay back in my native land where already the WSA had been functioning for several years, first in

Chicago, now in Washington, DC. However, before returning to the USA where I knew the "homestretch" awaited me, I was determined to try Israel once more.

The "mondialization" of the Jewish, Christian and Moslem holy sites, at least symbolically, was, I felt, essential to the whole future of the global movement. Armed with a US 3-month tourist visa on my stateless travel document, there should be no problem, I thought, in obtaining an Israeli tourist visa.

"Do you mean I just present the passport at Ben-Gurion and I enter just like that?" I asked amazed.

"Just like that," she replied laughing. "What do you think? Most of us were stateless at one time or another."

I marveled at the inconsistency. A mere change of documents and I would be welcomed into Israel. Same person, same ideas, same feelings, different label. Call yourself a "Palestinian" or a "Jew" or a "Moslem", or "Christian" or whatever, and depending on where you are in the world, you will be treated as either friend or enemy, either accepted as one of "us" or maybe shot as one of "them." Change the label and the attitude changes. And who condemned these relative labels as false, misleading and even blasphemous "Golden calves"? Why, the various spokespersons, i.e. prophets, of the divided religions themselves. Or the promoters of a political philosophy which united theretofore warring factions in the name of general welfare and "peace."

And if global peace was the goal, that philosophy could only be global.

"No press notice this time," I told Norman Pilkington, our WSA District II coordinator at whose home in North London, off Bayswater Road I was staying. "I prefer to enter just like that. No hassle. The main thing is to get in. The problems will no doubt come later."

"Right. Like when you try to fly the world flag at the Wailing Wall," he replied drily.

"Or maybe in front of the Church of the Holy Sepulcher," I added laughing. "Anyway, this time, no matter what, Toma and I will get the job done."

My diary notation while flying down the coast of France that day, January 12, 1977, revealed the depth of my feeling:

"At last, I'm on my way to the Holy Land! Again! Why? A World Citizen in the Holy Land! It makes sense. The land of the prophets, the Promised Land. But where are the prophets' representatives today? Are their voices stilled by the sound of tanks and the roar of warplanes? I possess two passports, both prophetic: the stateless and the worldly. What is the Middle East crisis? Do I have a solution for it? No, for there is no Middle East crisis. There is only a human crisis. And now that the Jews have their state, are they any more secure? Are they now happy? Was Israel the solution? Then why the fear, the insecurity, the army, the nuclear bombs? Is that what the prophets talked about?

"The Holy Land means consecrated to God, one God, not three or three hundred. The Holy Land by definition is spiritual world territory. And in the 20th century, its only promise is to spread to all the world community. This is the true meaning of Zion, the City of God. This is the mission of the Jews, to reveal by their words and deeds the global character of humans and humanity. For without this, neither they nor humanity will survive. The Jews are masters of survival. Throughout the centuries, they have learned how. Now is the Final Challenge."

BOAC Flight 576 arrived at Ben-Gurion airport at 6:50 p.m. The control girl looked perfunctorily at my stateless document, checked to see if the picture matched, smiled wearily, handed it back to me and said, "Next." My heart pounding, I walked onto the Holy Land.

Toma was waiting impatiently outside the barrier beyond the customs control benches; his long blond hair combed back, his eyes sparkling with their usual inner glee.

"So you made it at last," he said after bear hugs. "That's good. That's very good. Let's go quick before they realize what a mistake they've made!"

Toma had arrived with his Jewish mother in Israel from Budapest, Hungary in 1950 when he was 11 years old. At the age of sixteen, he decided three things: 1) He was not a Jew; 2) He was a vegetarian, and 3) he was non-violent. He also decided he wanted to be a world citizen, so he decided he was not a "national." His two legal battles, the first in Tel Aviv and the second, before the Supreme Court in Jerusalem to determine both his own religion and nationality, involve landmark decisions, not yet fully appreciated by the general citizenry.[11]

He became our WSA District Coordinator in 1975 after a visit to Chaggara on the way to a War Resisters International Conference in Brussels. Though we had different views on the basic meaning of government—he called himself a philosophical anarchist—I recognized in him a unique combination of virtues, not the least of which was a firm commitment to humankind and humane values. Fiercely independent, what many would call a "food freak" in his concern for what goes into what we eat; an environmentalist, "back to the simple life" advocate, fanatical human rights supporter, Toma possessed that rare detached, even visionary attitude which permitted a total commitment to what he held was right, good and true. In Israel, he was considered a maverick, a loner, and to some, a pain in the "tokus," but uncompromisingly honest. I liked him immediately. He was "married,"[12] with two teenage daughters.

"So what's on the agenda?" he asked me as we drove from the airport in his tiny Citroen.

"Just let me breath in this atmosphere," I returned, feeling a strange exhilaration unlike the first time I rode into Tel Aviv in the army vehicle six months before. Now I could freely enjoy the surroundings, the olive trees, the gently rolling hills, the multi-colored soil, despite the evidence everywhere of modern man, the highways, the construction, the debris, cars, cars, cars and inevitable gas stations.

"Enjoy, but not too much," Toma said soberly. "It can all disappear overnight." Brought back to reality by his gloomy remark and feeling an almost overwhelming sense of mission and urgency, especially in view of the promised upcoming campaign for world citizenship in the United States, I decided to visit Jerusalem as soon as possible. But first, I would try to see Abie Nathan in Tel Aviv.

The One and the Many

"I have tried to see Abie Nathan many times," said Toma, when I told him of my plans, "but he is always too busy." I smiled. Toma was controversial ever since his two trials. His uncompromising world citizenship plus his fervent advocacy of Israeli conscientious objectors as the Middle East representative of the War Resisters International, rendered working relationships with more conservative, if idealistic, Israelis difficult and often impossible.

I was thoroughly familiar with this problem. The world citizenship movement was composed of innumerable individuals who considered my personal affirmation of the civic status with world government as literally contradictory, therefore treasonable to their collective, organizational thinking. "Until we all declare world citizens together," their argument went, "no one individual can or should claim it." While I recognized in this argument the age-old dichotomy between the one and the many, I still knew personal identification was essential to the process of commitment to the many. The U.S. Founders were a classic example.

Toma was that rare human who refused to compromise on that personal identification. He was therefore "uncomfortable" to work with, being considered an iconoclast.[13] The day would come soon, I knew, when Toma's voice would be heard loud and clear in modern Israel as Abie Nathan's was already in a slightly different context. Both men were equally devoted to peace and human well-being and would one day recognize the other's worth in the common struggle. I could not hurry that delicate process.

"Who can wish to see you in Israel?" I asked him sternly. "You are worse than the Hasidic Jews. You are an active world citizen. Anyone who thinks in terms of Israel first, and the world second, will consider you their enemy. Poor Toma, you do not call yourself 'Jew' but you are a better follower of the ancient Jewish prophets than many who do. But do not worry about who will see you and who will not. Just react to what comes your way. You'll see. One day, no one will be able to resist you. Not even Abie."

Puzzled, but somewhat mollified, he dropped me off at Abie's apartment, arranging to meet me the next evening in Jerusalem.

After I recounted the events of the past six months from the time Israel "deported" me and he recounted his Peace Ship vs. Israeli government news, Abie telephoned a Ma'ariv correspondent who arrived within the hour. Though Ma'ariv was the government newspaper—the correspondent calling it "fascistic"—his article was surprisingly sympathetic largely due to the writer's personal bias for human rights.

Mission to Bahai Land

The following morning, I took a bus to Haifa to visit the Baha'i World Center and hopefully meet and talk with a member of the Universal House of Justice. Since my imprisonment in 1975 in Lucerne for 50 days when prominent Swiss Baha'i's gave me *Gleanings from the Writings of Baha'u'llah*, I was intrigued and inspired by the life and teachings of this latter day prophet.

"The earth is but one country, and mankind its citizens" is an article of faith of the Baha'i religion taught by him. I could embrace easily the thought that *"all men have been created to carry forth an ever-advancing civilization."*[14] Yet I could not reconcile this with another seemingly contradictory dictum: *"To none is given the right to act in any manner that would run counter to the considered views of those in authority."*

To Baha'is I would ask. "What of laws permitting killing? What of national armies? What of conscription? What of nationalism itself?"

The answers were unsatisfactory, always referring to this original command to obey those who "are in authority."

"But an American Baha'i could be looking down the barrel of a gun at a French, German or Russian Baha'i," I would point out. "Doesn't that contradict the world being one country and all mankind its citizens?"

"We are evolving world government through the Baha'i religion," they would answer. "In the meantime, we must obey all constituted authority even if it means going to war."

In Chicago, the year before, where we originally founded WSA's USA office under the capable direction of Kent Jones, one of Esperanto's leading exponents, Baha'i John Dale, a founding and board member, explained to me the dilemma of present-day Baha'iism.

"Although the chief principle of Baha'u'llah's teaching is the oneness and wholeness of the human race," he told me, "there is no one person today who can interpret that teaching in the light of excessive nationalism. You know that he urged the adoption of a world code of human

12

rights and responsibilities and even the creation of a world federal government. But Baha'is are not supposed to enter politics at all. You see, Baha'u'llah appointed his son, Abdu'l-Baha as a what he called 'The Center of his Covenant.' That means that any Baha'i could turn to Abdu'l-Baha on questions of interpretation of the teaching. Then at Abdu'l-Baha's death in 1921, in his will he appointed Shoghi Effendi, his eldest son, as 'Guardian of the Faith.'

"Under Shogi Effendi's direction, the Baha'is organized local Spiritual Assemblies which developed into the Houses of Justice. He lived in Haifa, our World Center, and was assisted by the International Baha'i Council. When he died in 1957, he did not appoint a successor as 'Guardian of the Faith.' So today, only the Universal House of Justice, composed of nine persons, selected by the local Houses of Justices, can interpret Baha'u'llah's teaching. But that leaves a lot of hard questions unanswered especially in view of the possibilities of nuclear war."

John Dale was a Baha'i *and* a citizen of the World Government of World Citizens. In his words, "I'm only following through on what Baha'u'llah taught. He said, *'Let your vision be world-embracing, rather than confined to your own self'* and *'That one indeed is a man who, today dedicateth himself to the service of the entire human race.'*

"Well, it seems to me that as a citizen of the World Government, no matter how few we may be at this point, I am really putting Baha'u'llah's teaching into practice. I cannot agree that as Baha'is we shouldn't mix in politics. We are already in politics as national citizens. And as Baha'is, we must have a positive and political response to being used as cannon fodder by our nations. Or else, it is all hypocrisy."

The bus trip from Tel Aviv to Haifa took only one and a half hours, the azure Mediterranean to my left, lapping peacefully on the sometimes sandy, sometimes rocky shore, and to my right, gently rolling hills interspersed with farms and orange groves. Traffic was heavy with big army trucks contrasting sharply with the tiny Fiats and Citroens.

As all visitors, I was greeted warmly at the Baha'i reception house by the inevitable question: "Are you a Baha'i?"

"Well, if being a Baha'i means working for the good of the world, then I am a Baha'i," I replied, remembering Abdu'l-Baha's words.

"But you do not belong to a local Baha'i church?"

"No." I sensed a slight cooling. "But I am a world citizen and I accept Baha'u'llah as a prophet."

Before the small temple where Baha'u'llah's remains are enshrined, a woman was handing to all comers a pamphlet explaining the significance of the shrine and instructing us to remove our shoes. Upon learning my name, she expressed delight at my visit. Encouraged, I asked her whether I might talk with a member of the Universal House of Justice.

"Why yes, I will ask my husband if he will have lunch with you," she replied.

Thanking her, I entered the beautiful room, lightly scented with the rose petals which were strewn carefully around the magnificent coffin in a small room, screened off by a thin veil. A sense of euphoria slowly overcame me as I stood silently in that sacred presence.

"The Tabernacle of Unity," Baha'u'llah had proclaimed in his Message to all mankind, *"has been raised; regard ye not one another as strangers. Of one tree are all ye the fruit and of one bough the leaves. The world is but one country and mankind its citizens...Let not a man glory in that he loves his country; let him rather glory in this, that he loves his kind."*

Standing here in this hallowed room on the consecrated ground of the Baha'i World Center, situated in the heights of the city of Haifa, in the sovereign state of Israel, I contemplated the stark contradiction of Shoghi Effendi's word concerning the *"animating purpose of the world-wide Law of Baha'u'llah"*:

"It calls for the wider loyalty, for a Super-State must needs be evolved, in whose favor all the nations of the world will have willingly ceded every claim to make war, certain rights to impose taxation and all rights to maintain armaments, except for purposes of maintaining internal order within their respective domains."[15]

How did these inspiring words compare, I wondered, with the nationalism, inflexible and creed-bound, of modern Israel? The modern state "tolerated" religion so long as it did not disturb the state's claim to absolute sovereignty.[16]

But was not God then the only Absolute Sovereign?[17]

In view of these explicit teachings, why did not the Universal House of Justice condemn nationalism, instruct young Baha'is not to enter armies, begin a worldwide political party with national branches which would elect legislators on the platform of world government and world citizenship, in other words, evolve *"some form of world Super-State...?"*

I would pose these questions to a member of the Universal House of Justice if we met for lunch.

A Global Paradox

"There is a small vegetarian restaurant just down the road," Dr. "Smith"[18] informed me after we had met at noon in the lobby of the splendid mansion in which the Universal House of Justice sat. He was in his early 50's, ruggedly handsome, friendly, bright-eyed with his generous mouth smiling at some secret joke.

After ordering two pita bread sandwiches with humus and apple juice, he asked me what was my mission in Israel.

I hesitated. To say that I wanted to "mondialize" the holy sites would be to include the Baha'i World Center. This might appear to be the height of presumption to a member of the Universal House of Justice. Furthermore, to declare that the World Center was "under the sovereign protection of world law" would be tantamount to defying Israeli state sovereignty.

On the other hand, neither the Israeli army, despite claims to the contrary, nor any national army could protect land on which holy sites were located. I remembered reading in one of Abdu'l-Baha's Tablets how *"in this day, means of communication have virtually merged into one. In like manner all the members of the human family have become increasingly interdependent. For none is self-sufficiency any longer possible, inasmuch as political ties unite all people and nations."*

This statement and others equally affirmative and declaratory, placed Baha'i in the forefront of political thinking among religionists. The key question then became, how do they confront the nationalistic powers-that-be that also affirm and declare absolute sovereignty?

"As a world citizen," I began, "I accept, as you do, the oneness and wholeness of the world community and humankind. This particular land, which can almost be called a shrine to that oneness and wholeness is today the scene of intense conflict and bitterness. I feel a personal affinity to all that has happened and is happening here. I share its anguish and its promise. The holy sites of all religions are in danger. They are God's territory. And there are not three gods or dozens. When I was asked six months ago at Ben Gurion airport when I first tried to come into Israel what was my religion, I had to reply 'monotheism.'"

He laughed. "That was a good answer. And what was the reaction?"

"Mostly bewilderment. They couldn't categorize me. I was out of the mainstream. Yet I was not a heretic either. I believed. Better yet, I accepted God's reality. Anyway, I want to visit the holy sites. As I have done today. I go to Jerusalem this afternoon. What will happen there I do not know. But I feel strongly that only world law can protect them from present danger."

"Yes, that is true," he said slowly, looking at me steadily. We ate for a moment in silence.

"Dr. Smith," I started, wondering how to breach the subject of obedience to constituted authority versus obedience to God's laws of unity taught and lived so eloquently by Baha'u'llah, "I am troubled by one aspect of the Baha'i religion. And I would be grateful if you would clarify it for me."

"Certainly," he replied, "if I can."

"It is the old contradiction between obeying God's or Caesar's laws. The Baha'is have gone further than any other religion in spelling out the need for a world government and I believe world citizenship is even a tenet of your faith."

"Yes indeed it is," he said quietly, his eyes slightly veiling.

"After I visited the Baha'i temple in Wilmette two years ago, I was taken to the home of a young Baha'i who had been a conscientious objector to war. But his position changed when he became a Baha'i. I found this strange. Even, well blasphemous, in view of Baha'u'llah's life and teachings. It was as if becoming a Baha'i sanctioned his killing. How do you explain this apparent contradiction?"

"It is a paradox," he said slowly. "I cannot deny that we are troubled by it."

I waited for more. Surely a member of the Universal House of Justice would have impeccable arguments supporting the duality of Baha'u'llah's teachings. I had imagined him bringing out that when the Master wrote about obeying "constituted authority," it was the 19th century when nationalism was a fountainhead of unity eliminating wars between smaller political factions.

On the other hand, his grandson, Shoghi Effendi, wrote that the principle of the 'Oneness of Mankind' as *"the cornerstone of Baha'u'llah's world-embracing dominion, implies nothing more or less than the enforcement of his scheme for the unification of the world.*[19]

I felt his anguish in his silence. What could he say, alone? He was a member of a council. He was not the 'Guardian of the Faith.'

My mind went back to my conversation with John Dale. The last 'Guardian of the Faith' himself had written that *"divorced from the institution of the Guardianship, the World order of Baha'u'llah would be mutilated and permanently deprived of that hereditary principle which, as Abdu'l-Baha had written has been invariably upheld by the Law of God."* Here was, unhappily, concrete proof of John's analysis.

The extraordinary irony of Shoghi Effendi's awareness of the vital necessity for a living interpreter of Baha'u'llah's Dispensation and his neglect to appoint a successor is further revealed in his own words:

"Without such an institution (Guardian of the Faith) the integrity of the Faith would be imperiled, and the stability of the entire fabric would be gravely endangered. Its prestige would suffer, the means required to enable it to take a long, uninterrupted view over a series of generations would be completely lacking, and the necessary guidance to define the sphere of the legislative action of its elected representatives would be totally withdrawn."

Dr. Smith finished his sandwich, drank from his glass, placed it deliberately on the table and looked at me somberly.

"All I can say is that there is a two-fold process at work in the world today," he began. "The first is essentially an integrating one; the second is disruptive. We Baha'is are primarily concerned with the integrative process. The other process tends to tear down, all by itself, the outmoded barriers that seek to block humanity's progress toward its destined goal. That is essentially why we remain divorced from politics."

I thought of my brother on the bridge of the USS Buck at Salerno helping to "tear down the outmoded barriers" with his life's blood. I thought of the bombs I myself dropped on German cities and tiny Belgian villages as part of the "disruptive process." I thought of the millions of exclusively national citizens, including "Dr. Smith," justifying the armies of latter-day Caesars in their blind determination to eliminate the human race once and for all.

Baha'u'llah, for all his grand mission, apparently did not foresee the nuclear peril. Nor did he envisage the day when instant communication and computers would permit the practical working of individual sovereignty on the world scale.

In "The Secret of Divine Civilization," Abdu'l-Baha, interpreting his father's teachings, outlining the future reorganization of the world, wrote that *True civilization will unfurl its banner in the midmost heart of the world whenever a certain number of its distinguished and high-minded sovereigns shall, for the good and happiness of all mankind, arise, with firm resolve and clears vision, to establish the Cause of Universal Peace."*

The "sovereigns" in this case, however, were not ordinary citizens but national leaders for he continues that *"they must make the cause of Peace the object of general consultation, and seek every means in their power to establish a Union of the nations of the world."*

The principle of collective security with its reliance on armed retaliation is thus clearly affirmed in that *"if any government later violates anyone of its provisions (the fundamental principle underlying 'this solemn pact') all the governments on earth should arise to reduce it to utter submission, nay the human race as a whole should resolve, with every power at its disposal, to destroy that government."*[20]

Dr. Smith apparently felt that I was not satisfied with his explanation for he asked me, perhaps out of politeness, "And how should a world citizen, according to you, act in the face of constituted authority?"

I took a deep breath. "Well, if that authority is serving both the general and individual good, then it should be obeyed. But if it is serving only a partial good at the expense of the general good, then a higher authority, on its own terms, should be invoked."

"And what do you mean by 'a higher authority'?" he asked intently.

I plunged on. "Well, citizenship and government are corollaries. Each world citizen is a microcosm of a world government, just as every national citizen is a microcosm of a national government, or should be. So a 'higher authority' would be simply a world government, but based on the sovereignty of each citizen, not of a collectivity; rather like a symphony orchestra."

"So how does that apply to military service?" he pursued politely.

"Well, the supposed reason for military service is security of the state because of the lawless condition outside the state. But the world citizen already exposes that reasoning as false since he embodies world law personally. When he adds the outer framework of world government, the state has no justification for drafting him." I recounted briefly the story of Fred Haas.[21]

"I see. Very ingenious." I decided having gone this far, I would risk going to the end of my thinking.

"If Bahai's are truly for world government and not merely a union of national states, then they should join the only world government now existent and help it evolve."

He smiled wanly but did not reply. The bill came and he paid. I thanked him for lunch, we shook hands and I left for Jerusalem.

Grand Tour

Toma and I left early Monday morning, January 17, for the Old City. My briefcase was bursting with the world flag, copies of the Universal Declaration of Human Rights, WSA pamphlets and world citizen application blanks.

I had been busy since leaving the Baha'i World Center at Haifa. The morning after arriving and checking in to an East Jerusalem hotel, I toured the Old City, visiting the Wailing Wall where I silently recited the "Shema Yisrael," then the Church of the Holy Sepulcher, entering a tiny room where, according to tradition, Jesus was buried,[22] and the Mosque of the Dome in the Moslem sector. Here I descended in the hollowed out cave below the rock on which Mohammed's footprint, according to legend, was stamped when he ascended to heaven. The calm within that holy place was transcendent.

Directly behind the Wailing Wall, still in the Moslem sector, within sight of the majestic Mosque, was a flat rock adjoining the concrete walkway from which a fig tree was growing. Weary from walking, I sat down for a while on this rock. As I stared at the huge gray stone of the ancient temple of David directly in front of me, a strange calmness overcame me.

Time passed. I was unaware of it. My contemplation seemed to scan eras and vast hordes of people, ancestors all. Prophets, sages, masters wove in and out of my thoughts. Their spirit became all-pervasive. The more I contemplated, the more I was drawn into the wonder of both timeless Truth and Time's inexorable dominion over all things material. I became literally "spaced out," immersed in euphoria, my body tingling as if each cell was being charged with a tiny cosmic battery permitting a higher vibratory rate. A sense of joyous belonging almost overwhelmed me.

On the 16th, Toma and I had visited the Palestinian refugee camp, Kalandia, on the road to Ramallah. A pitiful reminder of the 1948 war, it still contained 10,000 refugees living in small stucco bungalows facing dirt streets.

"For the first five years," the camp chief told us, "we lived in tents. But as they had to be replaced every two years and each tent cost $50. UNWRA[23] found it cheaper to put up these houses. Now we have been here almost 30 years. We dream only of returning to our own land and our own villages."

"But the villages don't exist anymore," I exclaimed. "You know they have been razed by the Israeli army. You can't return to bare rock."

"That is right. Our villages have been destroyed. But the land is still there. We will build again." His voice was steady, flat. The hate and fury may have been there, but if so, it was carefully hidden. Time, the great healer, could not eliminate memory.

I had studied the Zionist movement's history of Palestine which began with Theodor Herzl in 1897. As in all movements, there were "doves" and "hawks." The former such as Ahad Ha'am, Martin Buber, Judah Magnes, and Chaim Weizman, a president of the Zionist Federation, advocated peaceful coexistence and dialogue with the Arab population, while the latter, such as David Ben-Gurion, Golda Meir and Menachim Begin considered no basis of common interest with the native population possible. The Zionist objective, deriving from its philosophy of a Jewish "homeland", was the colonization of an already populated country.[24]

Given this objective, from its inception, the Zionist movement as such could not avoid aggression against the Arabs living in Palestine, just as the British could not avoid conflict with the indigenous Indians, or the Portuguese with the native Angolans, etc.

No less an authority than Defense Minister Moshe Dayan frankly admitted in 1968 the intent of Jews in Palestine.[25]

"We came to this country, which was already populated by Arabs and we are establishing a Hebrew, that is, a Jewish state here. In considerable areas of the country, we bought the land from the Arabs. Jewish villages were built in the place of Arab villages. You do not even know the names of these Arab villages, and I don't blame you, since these geography books no longer exist. Not only don't the books exist, the Arab villages are not there either."

What Dayan failed to state was that Arab land was bought from effendi feudal absentee landlords primarily interested in making money and the profits from "good" business. The Arab peasant was indifferent to who formally owned the land as long as he was not barred from using it. But expulsion from the land was precisely the Zionist objective and Kalandia was the living witness to that insidious policy.[26]

The chief and his staff all expressed immense interest in the WSA passport.

"At least we would have a document which identified us as Palestinians and not refugees," the chief said. We left a number of application forms with him and departed for Ramallah in the occupied Left Bank.

An Israeli soldier was stationed outside the home of Rawinda Tawel, the courageous and beautiful Palestinian journalist who wrote a series of articles exposing prison conditions for Palestinians. Recently released from prison herself, she was still under "house arrest."

"You must see our mayor, Karim Khalif," she told me when we were seated comfortably on her elegant patio drinking black coffee and munching on pastries sweetened with dates. "I think he should know of your ideas, though I must tell you, I think they are much too idealistic."

From her point of view, with the Israeli soldier within gunshot, the charge was well-founded.

"Remember," I told her, "I am stateless too, like you Palestinians. But whereas you only want to be Palestinians, I claim to be a world citizen. Of course, I am an American still. That can never change ethnically. But politics is today a game of global power and it can only be played realistically by world citizens whatever their ethnic background."

"I agree with you in principle," she replied, "but realities unfortunately do not always permit one to live by principles. But go see Khalif. You will like him. He is very open. He will see you."

The fiery mayor of Ramallah had given us an appointment for the afternoon of the 17th.

Now, on that morning, we were about to "mondialize" the most sacred sites of humankind.

Holy "Mondialization"

"Here is the spot," I said to Toma after we passed through the small gate separating the Moslem from the Jewish sectors.

"Oi, this is a very sensitive area," Toma replied anxiously. "Remember the guy from Australia who tried to burn down the Mosque of Omar last year. Well ever since then, they've doubled the guards. Positively no demonstrations are allowed."

"But we are not demonstrating," I said. "We're proclaiming."

"It's worse yet. For demonstrations, they just throw you in jail. For proclamations, they boil you in oil." He looked around uneasily.

"We'll see, I returned, laughing. "Now, let's take out the flag."

We fixed the flag between two briefcases. There were few passersby at this early hour.

"You'd better make your proclamation quick," Toma told me in a low voice, "here comes the first guard."

"But there's nobody here yet," I replied.

"And pretty soon even we won't be here if you don't hurry."

"O.K. In the name of the people of the world," I intoned firmly, "and invoking the blessings of all the masters, prophets, gurus and sages from time immemorial, I hereby declare these holy sites, all resting on the world territory, as God's sanctuaries, protected by the sovereign world law of world government."

"Hey, what's going on here?" The Palestinian guard came up eyeing the flag suspiciously.

"Nothing," I replied. "We're just standing here."

"But what's that flag?"

"That flag represents the one world in which we all live. The yellow border represents spirit or God or wisdom or truth and the figure inside the globe represents each human as well as humanity itself, and...."

"You're not allowed to make any demonstrations in this area," he said somewhat relieved that we appeared peaceable.

"Oh, we're not demonstrating." I replied. "You see, these holy sites are really in danger and we want to protect them. That's all."

"Danger? Danger from what?"

"From war."

"Oh, that. Well, just move on."

"Look, really. We're just standing here. We do not intend to do anything else. I imagine it's permitted to stand here."

"To stand yes, but not with a flag." But he was half smiling.

"Here, be a good chap. Take our picture, would you?" I asked, handing him my camera. We stepped back to either side of the flag. Asked to help some innocent tourists have a snapshot to send to the folks back home, a routine with which he was thoroughly familiar, he happily did as I requested.

A few passersby had stopped to look. Toma handed them a WSA pamphlet. That was enough for the guard. He left hurriedly to get reinforcements. The morning air was crisp, the sun at this time of year comfortably warming. We passed out our literature to a few tourists while waiting for the inevitable "fuzz" to arrive.

"Please, don't make trouble," the small Jewish captain said after we told him who we were. "That's nice, but if you're looking for people, go to the marketplace. There, you'll find plenty. Here it's forbidden to advertise whatever. Here is trouble. Just leave quietly. Now!"

There was no argument possible. "Trouble" meant anyone with an idea beyond sightseeing and praying. Handing out leaflets was "advertising." A flag was a symbol of possible insurrection. Or liberation. In any case, both were "trouble." He was waiting. I looked at Toma. He shrugged.

"O.K. I guess that's it," I said. "Anyway, the deed is done. Let's go." We folded the flag, picked up our bags and walked off happily.

The Associated Press, released by the local correspondent, Arthur Max, carried the story on the "A" wire worldwide:

JERUSALEM—Near the shrines of three great religions, Garry Davis unfurled the yellow, green and white flag of World Government and proclaimed the sacred sites of the Holy Land to be "under the protection of World Government."

"It was a symbolic declaration to show that there is no protection for any territory under the laws of nations," Davis said, who is the first self-proclaimed world citizen.

Davis raised his flag near Judaism's Wailing Wall, Christianity's Church of the Holy Sepulcher, and Moslem's Mosque of Omar. The sites are inside the old walled city of Jerusalem, a zone claimed by Israel, Jordan and Palestine, a zone which the Vatican wants to declare neutral and the United Nations wants to internationalize. It was therefore an apt spot to make a pitch for world government, Davis said.

Davis, 55, a former American, who renounced his citizenship in 1948 because he believed nationhood was outmoded in an era of instant communication, global economy and potential nuclear holocaust.

"The nation-state, which was created in the pre-industrial era was no more than a political fiction," Davis said in an interview, "so we founded a new political fiction called world government to which we give our sovereign allegiance."

A Brief History

I had had breakfast with Max, the AP journalist that morning at my hotel so he had the essential story but not the ludicrous aftermath on the Allenby Bridge recounted below. His story ended with a direct quote particularly apt I thought for my present location: "The national political system today is a house of cards and national citizenship is a collective suicide pact."

I had been recalling the tragic circumstance of the diplomatic meeting at Evian, France in the summer of 1938, a fateful year when Hitler invaded Austria and Chamberlain signed, in the name of Britain, France and Italy, the infamous "Munich Pact" condoning Hitler's partition of Czechoslovakia thus literally sanctioning the invasion of Poland one year later which triggered World War II.

The anti-Semitic laws followed close behind both occupations. Buchenwald concentration camp had already opened in July, 1937 and Dachau had opened four years before in March 1933.

The meeting at Evian, convened by President Roosevelt to discuss the fate of German Jews being systematically persecuted by Hitler's Nazi regime, was eclipsed by these cataclysmic events moving the world to war. Yet the results of the meeting—rejection by all 32 countries present of Jewish immigrants—have seared the pages of world history ever since.[27]

Hitler's "Final Solution" was effectively sanctioned by the nation-state closed system, represented by those craven and spiritless men who, as diplomats, accepted total dehumanization even in the face of monstrous injustices perpetrated in the name of nationalism gone mad.

The inevitable Holocaust has been used ever since, in dreadful irony, to justify the establishment, by whatever means, of another state likewise dependent on arms and armies for its apocryphal security.

To add a bitter historic twist to the irony, the Palestinians had become the "Jews" of the Jews.

Two "World" Mayors

Once outside the gates of the Old City, we hailed an "Arab Taxi" for Ramallah. We arrived at the Ramallah city hall at noon. A correspondent from the London Observer was interviewing the mayor.

As we waited in the small outer office, I noted an elderly man sitting on a bench to my right and gazing at me intently. When I smiled at him, he asked in a voice with a slight British accent, "May I know your name?" When I told him, he became extremely agitated.

"Now I know why I have been waiting all this time here," he said. "I had a 9 o'clock appointment with Brother Khalif but he said he could not see me today. It was a matter of no importance. But somehow I stayed on. This morning I opened my Bible to John 1(6) and somehow I knew I was to meet with someone today who walked with God. I am Constantin Quoffa."

"I am glad to meet you," I said. "We all walk with God if we but knew it."

"Yes, yes, that is true, but most do not know it," he replied sadly.

Constantin Quoffa was a Palestinian Christian living in Ramallah. A former customs officer for the British under the mandate, then retired, he was dispossessed of most of his property and living a hand-to-mouth existence with his large family in a small house on Ramallah's outskirts. His knowledge of the Bible was encyclopedic. He had a quote for every occasion.

"You must honor me by coming to my house for food after your meeting with Khalif," he said eagerly.

"We are delighted."

He left to prepare the visit.

The mayor's door opened and Karim Khalif, in his hearty, slightly accented voice, invited us to enter. As we entered his office at the city hall, a Voice of America journalist was coming out and a BBC man was waiting to do a radio interview.

Karim Khalif was definitely "in the world news."

"Please Mr. Davis, I want you to meet my good friend Muhammad Hasan Mulhim, the mayor of Halhul," he said, indicating a man in his mid-forties, wearing a dark brown business suit. "I wanted him to listen to your ideas." I was delighted that now two important West Bank mayors were on hand to receive Toma and me. Perhaps history would be made today.

After we were seated and the inevitable coffee served, Ms. Khalif asked me to explain the significance of world citizenship. I gave him a brief history of the movement since 1948, emphasizing the coincidence of the UN's declaration of human rights, the founding of the state of Israel and the subsequent war, and the beginning of the popularization of the ideas of world citizenship.

"It is the final application of the principle of self-determination, but for the entire race," I concluded.

"Ah, self-determination," he said. "We also claim self-determination, but you know the result." Mayor Mulhim nodded his head soberly.

"If you will allow me, Your Honors," I replied, "the principle of self- determination applied in a world of anarchy is tragically illustrated by the African states, which gained so-called independence from the colonial powers. Do they enjoy security today? Are their economic problems solved? Will the Basques or the Kurds, or the Todas or the Scots or the Bretons or any American Indian tribe gain security in the world as it is today if they achieve their own government? Will you Palestinians? There are 166 sovereign states now. Suppose there were 200 or 300? The world would still be threatened by war. And all those little states would be armed. What madness!"

"Are you then against Palestinian self-determination?" the mayor of Halhul asked solemnly.

"Not at all, on condition it takes place within the larger framework of human self-determination," I replied. "Otherwise, it will face the same problems as your neighbors who are pointing their guns at you. Their example should instruct you. Israel is now spending forty per cent of its budget on armaments and is running an eighty to one hundred per cent inflation."

Mayor Khalif shook his head as if clearing it. "There is much in what you say. But the problem is very complex here. There are many opposing forces and many opinions."

"Well, the one thing everyone agrees on is that you are Palestinians. And while the principle of self-determination of people is spelled out in international instruments, yet they say nothing about the definition of a people. That only means a given people must identify themselves. That is the first step to self-determination. And that's what I'm here for. The modern techniques of identity are by cards, passports, and other official documents. Now, you have Israeli identity cards and Jordanian passports. Who are you then? Nobody. But, I don't propose you make your own ID cards and passports because that would be to fall into the same error both Israel and Jordan have forced upon you. I propose that you become citizens of the World Government and thereby accept its ID and passport. Though they do not state a person's nationality, still the place of birth and the home residence are identified. You were born in Palestine, and you live, according to you, in Palestine. That is what you fill in on the application form. It is the beginning of self-determination, to identify yourself as you want."

I showed them my passport and World Government ID card. They studied it carefully, reading the back of the card slowly.[28] Finally, Mayor Khalif looked up with a smile.

"Good. I accept. I wish to become a world citizen."

"And I too," Mayor Mulhim added, "and I am happy to know such humane initiatives exist."

I turned to Toma who was getting out the application forms.

They filled them out and each notarized the form for the other. I asked if they would make a statement for distribution and they readily agreed.[29] They were delighted with the world flag and agreed to have their picture taken with Toma and myself holding it.

At the time of my meeting with Mayors Khalif and Mulhim, I did not discuss economics except to point out the highly visible inability of Israel to maintain itself economically without the giant infusion of capital from the United States, either governmental or from the Jewish population. A Palestinian state would also face horrendous economic problems largely unforeseen or deliberately soft-pedaled by those advocating Palestinian self-determination.

Few, with the exception of visionaries like economist Norman Kurland, had thought through to a new and revolutionary ownership strategy for the whole area, divorced essentially from land ownership which would result in economic freedom and well-being for each citizen, regardless of ethnic, religious or national affiliations.[30]

A Palestinian Christian and his Family

After warm good-byes with both mayors, we left the city hall with Constantin Quoffa, who was eagerly waiting to take us to lunch. As Toma had to return immediately to Jerusalem, I alone went with this dedicated Christian to his nearby home.

Constantin Quoff's 9-year-old son was sick in bed. His wan, beautiful face drew me irresistibly to his side. Quoffa's eldest son had returned that day from Baghdad where he was studying at the University. His wife and other sons and daughters were excited by both the return and my visit. But this little sick one was unable to participate. I touched his head to see if he had a fever.

"Are you a healer?" Constantin asked me wonderingly.

"I would like to be," I replied, thinking of what Frank Houghton Bentley, one of England's great healers, told me when I asked him if he would teach me how to heal. "There is nothing to learn," he had replied. "Just stretch out your hand. Anyone who wants to be a healer already is." Ever since then, when the occasion seemed right, I would "stretch out" my hand. Sometimes it "worked"; sometimes not.

The child opened his eyes and smiled up at me. Encouraged, I kept my hand on his forehead. (He was up and about the next day, Constantin later told me.)

"Lunch is ready," Mrs. Quoffa called from the other room. We went in to a copious meal. I recounted the meeting at the City Hall and the signing on of the two mayors as world citizens.

"Then you must meet the mayor of Bethlehem and also the City Manager of Gaza," Constantin told me. "We will go together. I have relatives in Gaza City. But I have no car."

"Then I will hire one for tomorrow," I told him. His son was eager with news about his university life in Baghdad.. He was studying to be an engineer. "Student life is very agitated now. Everyone is in politics and there are constant meetings. It is hard to study. Palestinians are considered outsiders. And our living conditions are very bad. There is not enough food and because of the overcrowded dorms, I have to share a bed with a night student. Can you get me into a university in America?" he asked me. Here again was a major problem for youth all over the world: too few universities, inadequate budgets for education and living conditions, and lack of teachers. The national budgets weighted towards armaments placed education on low priority when it should be near the top.

"Unfortunately, I have neither money nor influence in this department," I told him. "But keep in touch with me. Who knows? Maybe your destiny is to study in the United States. If so, you will not be able to escape it."

Bethlehem—World City

The following day, January 18th, in a rented Fiat, Constantin, Toma and I drove to Bethlehem toward the evening. Soldiers were everywhere, guarding the birthplace of Jesus Christ, Prince of Peace.

"We are here to prevent any disturbances," a young Israeli soldier told me when I expressed my shock at the military display outside the church built over the manger to which Mary was directed that fateful night.

"And who would disturb the birthplace of Christ," I asked naively.

He laughed harshly. "I can tell you have not been in Israel long. Today is Rosh Hashanah, the High Holiday for the Jews. Already there have been some incidents. We are here to protect you."

I looked at his automatic machine gun, ready at his hip. He was about 25 as were his mates, clustered at the military post.

"You chaps remind me of the modern version of the Roman soldiers guarding ancient Jerusalem," I said, trying to smile.

"We've heard that before," he returned coolly. "Have you come to make trouble or to see the birthplace?"

As the soldier's hands quickly went up and down my clothes searching for concealed weapons, I felt an almost uncontrollable fury building up inside me. It was all I could do to keep from striking him with all my might. The unspeakable indignity and more, the terrible irony of being suspected of violence upon trying to enter the very birthplace of Christ was to me symptomatic of the malignant disease afflicting all humanity, a disease Christ Himself exposed and for which He was crucified.

I recalled Thoreau's essay of civil disobedience: "Thus the state never intentionally confronts a man's sense, intellectual or moral, but only his body, his senses. It is not armed with superior wit or honesty, but with superior physical strength."

Here at this shrine where a God-man was born, who taught the power of Truth over error, who confronted the State with Higher Authority incorporated in his person, the State again, in modern dress, armed as never the Caesar's of ancient Rome could have dreamed, was mindlessly installed for "protection." Man, it seems, had understood nothing of Christ's teaching.

In a block of buildings on the square in which many brightly-lit stores sold plastic (Christ in the manger) sets, postcards and other memorabilia to eager tourists, we visited Mr. Freiss, Bethlehem's Christian Palestinian mayor in his 2nd floor apartment. Constantin Quoffa's reputation as a practicing Christian worked the magic of convincing the tired mayor to see us without an appointment on this festive yet threatening day. His attitude was cautious when Constantin introduced us as "world citizens."

"World citizens! That is something new. I am only a humble mayor of a tiny town in occupied Palestine. Why do world citizens wish to see me?"

"Your Honor, this tiny town is revered the world over as you know," I replied. "No temporal power can deny its transcendent status due to Christ's birth. Believe me, I feel as bitterly as you must about the stationing of soldiers around the birthplace of the Prince of Peace." His steady gaze changed subtly. Some of the searching wariness was replaced by a pensive, less guarded and slightly earnest regard.

"You are a Christian?" he asked me with a wan smile.

"No, not in the formal sense," I replied slowly. "I accept the power of wisdom to right wrongs. But I also know that law based on that wisdom is necessary. And since we are not all angels, I accept that such law must be enforced. If someone poisons the village well, that person must be punished. But the punishment should be redemptive. Not vengeful. I do not consider Christ's teachings mere pacifism. Turn the other cheek is good common sense."

"And how can I be of service to you as mayor of Bethlehem?" he asked with no trace of animosity.

"It is I who wish to be of service to you," I returned. "Yesterday, in the Old City, Toma and I declared the holy sites under the sovereign protection of world law. In 1949 in France, the city of Cahors declared itself 'mondialized,' that is, symbolically, it considered itself under the protection of a new world order.[31] In addition, it was saying to the government of France, that the State could no longer protect it in the 20th century. Many towns and cities have since made the same declaration, in Belgium, West Germany, England, Japan, Canada, and recently the United States. Three states in the United States – Iowa, Wisconsin and Minnesota – have made similar declarations. Bethlehem is already a world town. It belongs to humankind. As do all places where saviors and prophets were born and died. We propose that Bethlehem accept the Charter of Mondialization."

I passed him the document to which so many mayors and municipal councils had already affixed their signatures.

He took it gingerly. I could almost read his thoughts. "The idea is interesting...but dangerous. We are presently occupied. What would the Israelis think...and do? But in any case, I cannot reject any worthwhile idea that promises a surcease to our present untenable predicament."

"Thank you, Mr. Davis. I will study these documents carefully. And now, if you will excuse me, it has been a long day."

We three took our leave and returned to Constantin's home, planning to visit Gaza City the following morning to see the City Manager, Mr. Shawwa, cousin of the famous mayor of that tortured place.

A Precious Gift

On the way to Gaza the next morning, just before reaching Atarot Airport on the Ramallah-Jerusalem road, Constantin asked me to take a dirt road on the right leading upwards. The passable road finally ended on the crest of a hill overlooking the tiny, one runway airport and afforded a magnificent panorama of the surrounding countryside. A low stone wall ran along the crest for about 50 meters at the end of which was a small house in construction. The wildness and the height, accentuated by the cool breeze, were exhilarating and I felt wonderfully at home.

"Here I own a piece of land," Constantin said. "You see, behind this wall extending for ten durum below and along the crest of that house. If you want, I will give to the World Government a part of it, ten by ten durum."

I was speechless. A piece of land in the Holy Land! "Owned" by the World Government. I did not anticipate what legal problems were involved or even if such a land transfer was possible given the circumstances of occupation. Already, the Knesset had extended the boundaries of Jerusalem at Ararot Airport calling it "Greater Jerusalem." Whether its extension included Constantin's property I did not know. I would try to see Teddy Kolek, Jerusalem's peripatetic and ebullient mayor, on the morrow to find out.

However, the details did not matter to me at the moment. I was thinking of a tiny parcel of Holy Land being declared "world territory," a parcel which, unlike the historic holy sites and unlike the human habitations, was open to the sky, untouched by human hands, maybe trod upon by the prophets, God's earth, no more, no less. I knew a durum was about 1 by 1 meters.

"This is a wonderful gesture, Constantin," I told him. "Whatever happens, I accept in the name of all world citizens."

We climbed the wall to stand firmly on the land. "Here, from the end there." He pointed to the left where the open crest was stopped by foliage, then dropped off sharply. "We will measure off ten durum. I have all the papers at home. All my land has been expropriated but this."

Toma remained skeptical. "The Israeli government will not allow foreigners to possess land here. Land is the main thing. Every inch is contested."

"We could make a private agreement between Constantin and say, the World Service Authority as a legal corporation. Vis-à-vis the Israeli government, the land would still be his."

"It would be nice to have a small office here," Toma mused, gazing over the peaceful scene.

Gaza Welcome

Mr. Shawwa greeted us in the presence of three members of his municipal council. He called the ideas "appealing" but remained non-committal as to whether they could be applied to Gaza. He was cordial and I felt not personally unreceptive. I recounted our meeting with mayors Khalif and Mulhim, at which his eyes grew wide.

"So our brothers are already citizens of your world government," he said in some wonderment.

"We have been receiving letters from all over the world from Palestinians asking for our documents," I replied. "Like the Jews, they are now spread to all the corners of the earth, and often they face problems with the local authorities."

At my linking the problems of the Jews with Palestinians, he grew uneasy. From his vantage point, with over 200,000 Palestinians squeezed into a territory the size of Rhode Island, controlled tightly by the Israeli military, the comparison was, if not odious, at least strained. However, he also agreed to study our documents on mondialization, and we departed with the traditional, "Salaam."

His Honor of Jerusalem

Abie Nathan had advised me to walk into Teddy Kolek's office cold. "He is a very informal guy," he said. "Very regular. If you try to go through his secretary, you might never get to see him. Just walk in and tell him you're from Washington, DC. That's the 'New Jerusalem.'" He was right. When I presented my World Service Authority card to Mayor Kolek's secretary the next morning, January 20th, with its Washington address, she took it in immediately to the busy chief executive of perhaps the world's most historic city, certainly its most contested.

"Such a famous man!" he exclaimed as he came bursting from his office in his shirt sleeves. I was taken aback by the unexpected greeting as we shook hands.

"I bring you greetings from Leo Freudberg from Washington," I said.

"Nice. Leopold Freudberg is a good friend of Israel. His daughter lives in Tel Aviv. So what brings you to Israel, Mr. World Citizen?"

"I'm on a pilgrimage. Ever since 1948 I have wanted to come here...."

"As a Jew?" he asked smiling.

I hesitated. The question contained a whole world of meaning. My ancestors on my father's side, coming from Riga, Latvia and Vilna, Russia, would unhesitatingly have answered yes. My ancestors on mother's side from England, Scotland and Wales would have answered no. Mother came from Congregationalist New England, her ancestors, the Hodgkins and Emerys, arriving from England in the early 17th century.[32] Solomon Davis, my great grandfather left Russia for America at 18 in 1860 to escape conscription into the Russian army while his father, David Meyer Schlaberbersky had already arrived in the New World in the late 18th century driven out by pogroms in Latvia.[33]

So, what was I? I had been confirmed at the age of 16 at Keneseth Israel, a reform temple in Philadelphia. On the other hand, every school day from age 13 to 17, I had attended chapel at Episcopal Academy to say the Lord's prayer and the Nicene Creed with the rest of my schoolmates. I do not recall being especially uncomfortable with either locale except for the gnawing suspicion that God did not sanction the obvious split. My parents, conforming to the liberal notion of education in that epoch, did nothing to enlighten me or, as far as I know, my brothers and sisters as to our specific religious identity. I assumed therefore that I had none. However, what impressed me more than religious prayers, whether Jewish or Christian, was a "Moral Code for School Children" printed on a scroll like the Ten Commandments hanging outside the bathroom on the 3rd floor of our home in Philadelphia. There was no way to avoid it at least three times a day. This is where I learned the "Cleanliness is next to godliness" and "Justice is the true companion to Peace" aphorisms.

"No, not specifically," I replied to Mayor Kolek's innocent yet complex question. "That is, not as an immigrant. But as a world citizen which, in a way, I think, all Jews are."

I noticed I was not being invited into his office. Well, no matter, I would say what I had to say standing there in the antechamber.

"Mr. Mayor, Jerusalem, as you well know, is what might be called a 'world city,' truly belonging to all peoples in a historical sense."

His eyes narrowed. This was a delicate issue, one on which he was firmly positioned. No doubt others before me had discussed the "open city" concept with His Honor. However, I was sure no one had proposed that Jerusalem be "mondialized." Nor was I about to do so directly. I only wanted to introduce the subject. Jurist Luis Kutner, "Chief Justice," of our Would Government court, would have called it "constructive notice." Sensing his reluctance to discuss this sensitive issue, I decided to seek the information about Constantin's land offer before he brushed me off entirely. "But first, I have a technical or maybe legal question to ask you."

"So ask."

"A Mr. Constantin Quoffa, who lives in Ramallah, has offered our non-profit corporation a small piece of land just beyond the Atarot Airport. May the organization own the land, and secondly, may we put a building on it?"

"If it belongs to Mr. Quoffa, he cannot sell it to a foreigner or to a foreign company. Secondly, as to the building, if it is in what is called the 'green zone,' then he can build on it."

Mr. Kolek's attitude had undergone a subtle transformation at the mention of Constantin Quoffa. He knew from the name that he was a Palestinian; he also knew he was a Christian. The invisible line between "them" and "us" was unmistakably manifest in his new coolness. Since I was not on the "us" side, I was obviously one of "them." The interview, I felt, was fast coming to a close.

"Thank you for the information, Mr. Mayor. Just one more thing." I took from my briefcase the documentation on mondialization.

"May I ask you to have a look at these when you have a chance? I have had the privilege of speaking with many mayors in many countries, and as all cities throughout the world are bound together by common needs and a common destiny, we claim they share a common cause. These papers are simply an explanation of that cause and how certain municipalities have reacted to it."

He took the papers without enthusiasm. "I will have a look," he said non-committally.

"Good-bye, Mr. Davis and Shalom."

A Parcel of Mother Earth

I drove immediately to Ramallah with Toma to fetch Constantin. Together we proceeded to his land above the airport. I had alerted the UPI and AP correspondents in Jerusalem that at 3 p.m., I would be dedicating a piece of the Holy Land as "world territory." Another ceremony,[34] however, in far-off Washington, was dominating the news[35] and no media showed up.

Toma had arranged some rocks on our tiny patch of land in the shape of the world with a human figure stretched inside. I took the world flag from my briefcase and attached it to a pole. The fitful breeze caught it, and with Toma and Constantin standing to one side, with no one else to hear, but determined to speak the words nonetheless, I intoned to them and the world's wind:

"By the authority vested in me as a sovereign world citizen, speaking in the name of each and every fellow world citizen as well as in the name of humankind, I hereby declare this land 'World Territory' consecrated already by the words and deeds of all the martyrs to peace, freedom and justice who once walked and lived here. From this day forth, this land shall be under the sovereign protection of world laws deriving from the one God Who has dominion over all."

Toma was not happy with my invocation of the deity. A self-proclaimed atheist, he equated God with religion and religious attitudes. His entire life, however, was for me a living prayer. I was in no way perturbed by our seeming differences. If God was good and wise, I could as easily accept "goodness" and "wisdom" instead of the word "God." And I fully agreed with Toma that "God" was a powerful word which was often used to transfer money from one pocket to another. Or temporal power from one despot to another.

Constantin's neighbor, watching the ceremony from his half-built house, came along just in time to take a picture of the three of us after which we all went to his house for a friendly coffee.

The Line

I returned the rented car to Jerusalem, packed my belongings, said good-bye to Toma, and took an Arab taxi back to Ramallah to prepare for my exit from Israel via the Allenby bridge frontier with Jordan.

Constantin would accompany me to Jericho and the Israel frontier by taxi. Then after being controlled, we would board a bus for the Jordanian frontier and Ammon. Since I had no visa for Jordan but would have an exit stamp on my stateless document from the Israeli authorities, I could not present that document to Jordanian border guards. Once I had left Israel, therefore, I would have to travel only with the World Passport. I did not anticipate the ludicrous situation this would cause for me.

As we approached the biblical town, Constantin pointed out to me the hills to our left.

"It was there that Christ was tempted by the devil," he said.

Directly below, nestling in the foothills extending to the plain, was a large camp of tents.

"That was once a refugee camp," he continued, following my gaze. "It was full after the 1967 war. Now there are only a few living there. They refuse to leave."

After passing through the ancient town, we arrived at the frontier at 11 a.m., Friday, January 21st. We passed one barrier a few miles east of Jericho on a seemingly deserted road. A gate was half-ajar and a barbed wire fence stretched in both directions. We passed through and the road became winding with dunes on both sides.

"Everything is mined from now on," Constantin said, "except the road of course." We arrived finally at the hectic frontier post. Buses were lined up beyond the covered gates, like a racetrack, at which specific categories of humans were to present themselves: Palestinians with Jordanian passports; visitors with foreign passports; UN personnel.

I did not fit.

I stepped up to the window marked "UN Personnel." My stateless passport was perused and stamped for exit. Constantin was already on the next outgoing bus. I hopped aboard and found him toward the back. The bus was full mostly with Palestinians and a few UNWRA personnel. We started up and had gone but ten yards when the bus stopped. A red barrier blocked the road. The door opened and an Israeli soldier climbed aboard. "Control," he said curtly. We had been given small slips of paper by Immigration to turn over to the military. So, we were now in the military zone. Jordan was still technically at war with Israel. As the soldier came up the aisle, everyone nonchalantly turned over his slip of paper. I did also. Everyone passing Israeli military inspection, he got out, the door closed and we continued. The road wound more than ever. Now gun emplacements were visible, jutting out from what appeared to be sand dunes. Finally, on a hill to my left, I saw an Israeli flag flying the Star of David, the same David who wrote:

"The earth is the Lord's, and the fullness thereof; the world and they that dwell therein."[36]

We arrived shortly thereafter at the Allenby Bridge. It was unimpressive. Wooden, all of 30 feet long, it spanned the Jordan River at a point where it was no more than a stream. A small Israeli post with several lounging soldiers was placed about 15 feet from the bridge; the Jordanian frontier post was a small building directly at the bridge's end.

I put my stateless document in my pocket as the bus rattled over the bridge.

"If I don't get through," I told Constantin, "call the Associated Press in Ammon and tell them I am stuck on the Israeli-Jordanian frontier."

The bus stopped at the bridge's far side. A Jordanian sergeant came aboard. He was about the same age as the Israeli soldier, I thought. They were "enemies," yet performed the same function, maybe ten times a day.

"Everyone without a Jordanian passport, come with me for passport control," the sergeant said in a gruff voice.

I descended with about five others and entered the building. We seated ourselves around a small table behind which the sergeant sat. Passports were handed to him, one by one. Finally I handed over mine, I thought, just as casually as the others. He paged through it impatiently after checking the photo. No visa.

"You will not enter Jordan. No visa," he said handing it back.

"But I'm just transiting from Jordan to Khartoum," I replied, "then back to the States."

"You are returning to Israel. You cannot enter Jordan," he intoned. The others appeared embarrassed for me. They moved restlessly.

"I am returning to Israel? But what have you to do with Israel? I thought you were Jordanian."

"I am Jordanian," he said angrily.

"But then how can you speak for the Israelis?" I returned calmly.

"Enough of this," he said rising. To the others, "You may continue." To me: "You. Do you have any luggage?"

"Yes, of course. But listen, at least telephone Ammon for instructions. My passport is sanctioned by the Universal Declaration of Human Rights. Here is a Jordanian visa on it already." I showed him a photocopy of the visa affixed on a world passport mailed to us a year before.

"Come," he said, getting up, "it is 12 o'clock and Friday, Shabath. There is nobody working now in Ammon. And I cannot give visas. Get your luggage."

The driver retrieved my suitcase from the top of the bus. Constantin tried to get off the bus with me. I shoved him back on quickly. "No, go on to Ammon," I told him, "and relay the message I gave you." The bus door closed and it pulled away in a cloud of dust.

Three soldiers surrounded me. "All right gentlemen," I said, "now please show me where Jordan ends."

"What do you mean, where Jordan ends?" the sergeant inquired.

"Well, you have said I can't enter Jordan, So I suppose that means that you must put me out of Jordan. Well, to do that, we have to find out where Jordan ends, don't we?"

He looked at me coldly. "Jordan ends in the middle of the bridge."

"OK, that's more like it." I picked up my suitcase. "Let's go."

We all moved onto the bridge and quickly arrived at Jordan's actual frontier. I stopped.

"Here?" I said pointing downward to the bridge.

"Yes," he replied.

I took one step further.

"OK, Now I'm out of Jordan. Salaam."

The soldiers looked at the sergeant. He just stood there looking increasingly frustrated. From the other side of the bridge, an Israeli sergeant was rapidly approaching.

"What's going on here?" he asked brusquely to his fellow "enemy" sergeant.

"He is refused entry into Jordan. We are returning him to you."

"Hey, wait a minute," I said sharply, "I am no longer in Jordan. You said so yourself. But I am not yet in Israel. I'm on the line between the two countries."

"What line?" the Israeli sergeant asked in asperation..

I sighed. I had found it self-evident that for two distinct, separate nations to exist side-by-side, there was obligatorily a physical dividing-line between them. Whether that line was natural, like a mountain, a river or an ocean, it had to exist actually in order to provide the "reality" of two "sides." What was overlooked, like the nose, was that this line could not belong to either side. It had to be neutral territory. Otherwise, neither side could pretend to be distinct from the other.

Taking out my world passport, I turned to the Israeli sergeant. "Tell me, can Israel accept a person against his will?"

"Of course not," He replied hotly. "We are a democratic country."

"Fine, then I remain here, on the line between your two countries. Besides neither of your countries recognize my passport anyway." I held it up.

They stared at me, then at each other.

Finally, the Jordanian burst out, "But you can't stay here. It is impossible."

"Well, it may be unusual, but I really have no choice. You see, this is a point of international law. It is no longer a military question. There are many international instruments to support my position. You'd better get some advice."

"But you cannot stay on the bridge," the Israeli protested.

"Why not?" I asked calmly.

"Because…because," he sputtered. "It gets dark at night."

"That I know," I returned.

"It is dangerous" he went on. "From now on, there will be no civilians, only soldiers. And when it gets dark, sometimes there is gunfire."

I could not help laughing.

"That is interesting," I said finally. "During the day, you chaps cooperate with each other in controlling us civilians, and at night you shoot at each other."

The Jordanian sergeant looked at the Israeli sergeant who returned his puzzled gaze.

Finally, the Israeli sergeant said, "This is a military area. We cannot be responsible for your safety."

"Well, if you insist on killing each other shooting across the bridge, I guess you'll just have to shoot through me," I told them. "But don't worry. I am unarmed. I can't shoot back. You see, I'm for peace."

Both soldiers remonstrated hotly.

"What do you think we are doing here if we do not want peace?" the Jordanian sergeant shot back.

"It is you who are causing all the trouble," returned the Israeli sharply.

"Listen to me, both of you," I said with rising anger. "Before both of you were born, I was a soldier dropping bombs on civilians in World War II. I know your foolish game forwards and backwards. You are both about the same age. How many young people do you think there are in the world in different uniforms ordered to kill one another. And for what? A piece of the earth's surface, Lebensraum? A place in the sun? You think you belong to different states. You think you oppose one another. But here now, on this bridge you are supposed to be guarding, you know the truth. I spoil your phony game because I am standing on a line between you you can't touch. Because it doesn't belong to either of your states. It belongs to us, the world's people. It is like an equal sign between two sides of an equation. You do not bring security to your own citizens. That is your illusion. You bring only death and destruction. Peace means unity, not division, which your uniforms represent. If you really want peace, drop your guns, take off your insignia and join me on this line. This is the only peaceful territory here!"

They were astonished at this outburst. I thought I had gone too far when I saw the Israeli's finger tighten on his submachine gun. Finally, he said curtly, "Where is the document which allowed you to leave Israel."

"That cannot concern you any longer." I replied coldly, "since I am no longer in Israel. The only document I will show you now is the world passport." I held it up to him.

"We do not recognize this document," the Jordanian said quickly.

"It is not my responsibility if Jordan refuses to recognize a document sanctioned by the Universal Declaration of Human Rights," I said to him. "Yet I remind you, Sergeant, that Jordan, as well as Israel is a bona fide member of the United Nations from which this Declaration is sanctioned."

"But all you have to do is give us the other document," wailed the Israeli. He was now joined by a captain.

"We have no time for this nonsense," the newcomer barked. "If you refuse to give us this document, we will take it by force."

"That would be a very serious violation of my rights, Captain," I returned calmly. "First, it would be an assault on my person without due process. Second, you would operating outside of Israel proper. I would think twice, sir, before making arbitrary decisions. You just might be surpassing your authority." I smiled innocently.

The Jordanian turned on his heels angrily and stomped off. "He is now your problem."

The Israeli captain glared at me, his lips in a tight line, then turned and marched off to the telephone inside the post.

Finally, blessedly, I was alone in the middle of Allenby Bridge. The sun was shining brightly. I felt extraordinarily calm yet as if a coiled steel spring was inside me ready to explode if slightly triggered.

After half an hour, the captain returned, a grim smile on his lips. "I have orders from Jerusalem to remove you from the bridge. Now, will you please come with me?"

"Your orders may have been to remove me, but they didn't say I had to cooperate. I have my orders too. And they don't include being forced into a country against my will."

"Very well. If you refuse to cooperate, you must face the consequences." The infamous threat of national soldiery. "If you don't evacuate your villages, we will burn them down. Then you will be responsible for the burning." In brief, surrender to our threat of violence or else, suffer the violence. The "choice" is yours.

I did not reply. He motioned to his soldiers. I sat down on the bridge. Three of them could not lift me, mainly because they did not want to. The indignity and humiliation was too great...for them. The psychology of non-violent resistance has been fully detailed elsewhere. Frustrated, the Israeli returned to his telephone. In ten minutes, a bus came rumbling to the bridge from the Jordanian side. What a marvelous example of collusion, I thought to myself. The Jordanians sent a bus to help the Israeli's get rid of a "peacenik." I wondered how far up the Israeli chain-of-command it had to go to plead with Jordanian officials to reconnoiter a bus from the "enemy's" side. The bus stopped directly in front of me.

"This is your bus," the captain said inanely.

"No, this is Jordan's bus," I replied, remaining seated. He gave an order in Hebrew. His soldiers bumped me aboard like a sack of potatoes, cursing me out for not being a "gentleman."

Off we went to Jericho.

In the Jericho police station, after a half-hour interrogation from an Israeli civilian police chief, who first pleaded, then cajoled, then threatened, in trying to get me to give up my stateless travel document on which the exit visa had been stamped.

"But captain, don't you understand," I replied, "I have been brought into Israel by force, illegally. I am literally your prisoner. Yet, I am not charged with any crime. I left your country legitimately. Your demand is irrational. You kidnap me from outside your country, then ask me politely for a travel document while I am your captive. That's called 'coercion.' What kind of a country is this anyway? I know the law, and what you are doing is highly illegal."

He gruffly ordered me out of his office to the reception room where two officers began going through my luggage after having searched me thoroughly. While waiting on the Allenby Bridge, I had slipped the travel document to my camera case, which was now by my side. The officers were busily going through the suitcase. I carefully unzipped the case and furtively shoved the document around my back and under my jacket. Later, I thought, when I went to the bathroom, I would insert it under my pants held by my belt, I knew that eventually it would be found, but I would play out the absurd scenario to the end.

When they had exhausted the luggage, they asked me for my wallet. I gave it to them and everything came out including my calling cards and the article from Ma'ariv and the AP story about the mondialisation of the holy sites. They both read them eagerly, then looked at me in bewilderment and growing consternation. One went hurriedly to the telephone. He dialed at least six numbers, reading the articles excitedly each time. I was certainly becoming known in government circles.

At five o'clock I was hauled up, half-carried to a waiting police van, my luggage following. The trip from Jericho is one from below sea level to 2600 feet above, from warmth to cold. As we neared Jerusalem, detouring around the Old City on Ha-ofl Road, we passed the Garden of Gethsemanee to our left.

Well, I thought to myself, at least we were both on the same side of Caesar's law.

The Nation's "Solution"

The Jerusalem City Jail is more like an armed fortress than a prison. We passed through three checkpoints before arriving finally at the "reception." A swarthy-looking guard in a rumpled officer's uniform approached me after I put down my suitcase.

"Now here, Davis, we do not fool around. I am from Morocco. I was in charge of the prison there. I know all the tricks. You have a travel document. I want it. If you give it to us, there will be no trouble. If you do not, we will get it anyway. So what is it to be?"

"I cannot cooperate with you because I am not legally in Israel. My very presence here is in violation of my rights."

"I know nothing about your rights. I know only my orders. So..." With that, he started roughly stripping off my shirt and undershirt. Pushing me to the floor, my pants were next. He arrived inevitably at the document stuck into the back of my shorts.

"Aha! So you try to trick us?" he said triumphantly holding up the document for all to see. I shrugged, pulling up my pants. He handed it to an officer at the desk who in turn handed it to a runner who scampered out the massive door.

He returned in half an hour and handed me my document. "You are free, Mr. Davis. You can go."

"Can I go back to Allenby Bridge from where you brought me?" They laughed uproariously.

"Mr. Davis, take some good advice," said the man who had searched me. "Go home and go to bed. It is Shabath."

I looked into the travel document. Some Hebrew words had been scribbled over the exit visa. I did not even rate a rubber stamp, I thought.

I was escorted out of the prison labyrinth in a police van.

"Hey, Davis," the driver called after me as I walked away on the Jerusalem street to find a taxi for Tel Aviv. I turned around angrily.

"Shalom!" he said with a laugh.

That night, in a small hotel in Tel Aviv, I considered my unique situation. Where was I now, in Israel or simply in the Holy Land? The Israeli government had literally kidnapped me from outside its alleged territory. Then it had violated my person and forcibly taken a document from me in a prison. Then I was "freed." So, what was my status in Israel? To me, the Israeli government, by torturing its own laws in my regard, rather, by suspending them, was obliging me to exercise the "right of self-government." I could sympathize with Thoreau who, upon being locked up in a Concord local jail for not paying his income tax, wrote that *"I could not but smile to see how industriously they locked the door on my meditations, which followed them out without let or hindrance, and they were really all that dangerous."*[37]

I would have the chance to test my own sovereignty upon leaving from Ben-Gurion airport on the 24th for London. The irony of having been refused entry into Israel with my WSA passport on my first try, then having been forced into Israel without showing any documents, would now be compounded when I left, or tried to leave—as tight a security control as upon entering— with only my WSA passport.

And if I refused to present my stateless document again, would the police again take it from me by force, or would they refuse to allow me to leave, thus in effect forcing me to remain in Israel?

"I was not born to be forced," wrote the sage of Walden, and *"A very few, as heroes, patriots, martyrs, reformers in the great sense, and men, serve the State with their consciences also, and so necessarily resist it for the most part."*

I would be resisting the State's demands at Ben-Gurion Airport as it had resisted mine in "no-man's land" in the middle of Allenby Bridge.

"I am too high-born to be propertied,

33

To be a secondary at control,
Or useful serving-man and instrument
To any sovereign state throughout the world. "[38]

In compliance with protocol and as a matter of record as well as my interpretation of them plus a strategic power "tool," I decided that the President of Israel should be informed of the events of the past two days. Also, the letter would prove useful when the chief security officer at Ben-Gurion Airport reacted to my refusal to present docilely the now gimmicked stateless travel document at his "official" demand.

After outlining the relevant facts, I concluded that "this is to inform you, Mr. President, that I consider myself no longer within the territorial jurisdiction of Israel and that my only document of identity relating to my status is my WSA passport, a World Government document, grounded in the Universal Declaration of Human Rights."

The letter was mailed the 23rd with a copy to the United Nations in Geneva.

A Global Exit

Toma accompanied me to the airport while I briefed him on the incident on the bridge, its consequences and now my plan, showing him my letter to the president. He read it laughing

"You're a better anarchist than I am," he said.

"Not at all," I answered. "Just a determined and playful world citizen."

"It's almost the same thing," he returned brightly as we drove into the parking area.

I checked my bags through and presented my ticket to the young woman in uniform at the street level.

"May I see your passport, please," she said politely. She paged through the global document seeking the non-existent entry visa.

"But did you enter Israel with this document?" she asked puzzled.

"No, but I am leaving with it," I smiled sweetly.

She looked at me suspiciously. "Just a moment, please."

Like an electric current passing from light bulb to light bulb, the other women in the other posts stopped to look. They were hypersensitive to trouble, I thought to myself. Anything out of the ordinary was trouble. I remembered when flying a B-17 how my eyes would automatically flick across the instrument panel with its dozens of dials every thirty seconds or so. If the slightest deviation had occurred, I would instantly notice it. Humans can be "triggered" to respond instinctively to "abnormal" behavior by a rigorous conditioning process, sometimes subliminal, without the reasoning mind involved at all. Try looking at a police officer, then look around furtively as if trying to escape, then run away. Without thinking, he may draw his gun and shoot.

"Will you please come with me," the woman asked, handing me back my passport.

"O.K. Toma, this is it. Keep their feet to the global fire. Shalom and Salaam."

We hugged each other and I followed the woman upstairs to control headquarters.

"Where is the document with which you entered Israel, Mr. Davis?" the chief security officer asked me sourly.

We looked at each other. What a foolish comedy, I thought. Grown men confronting each other over a document. The man in front of me, my brother human, no doubt a father and maybe even a grandfather, facing me with the same dangers, frustration and final destiny, were locked in a modern drama where he was cast in the role of defender of the artificial frontiers of statehood and I was defending the seamless whole of the world community. He could not relish his part, I thought, since, being Jewish, he already accepted the oneness of God and therefore, the essential oneness of His creation. Well, the show must go on as the saying goes on my beloved Broadway; the curtain is up on the final scene of this modern tragic but illustrative documentary.

"In my inside jacket pocket," I replied coolly.

"Will you please give it to me" he asked.

"No." He stiffened. I looked him directly in the eye. "I will not resist if you take it by force." I told him, "but if you do, you must be prepared personally to accept the consequences."

"The consequences? What consequences? Are you threatening me?" he shot back angrily.

He needed some calming down, I thought. "Perhaps you had better read the letter I addressed to your president yesterday," I said, taking a copy from my pocket. "It has also been distributed to the press."

He took it skeptically yet with a hint of eagerness. Maybe it would get him off the hook. After reading it, he gave me quick startled glance, then returned to his office and picked up the phone.

A young, visibly distressed man in a dark suit approached me.

"Mr. Davis," he began petulantly. "We are off-loading your baggage. You seem to be in some kind of trouble with security and we...."

"Just a moment," I cut him off sharply. "Who are you?"

He was somewhat taken back by my curt manner, but recovered. "I am the BOAC manager here," he replied haughtily.

"And I am a paying customer," I shot back. "Now I advise you to drop that insolent tone of voice with me, and secondly, I advise you to get my bags back on board immediately. I am leaving for London on that flight." His mouth opened and shut. He hesitated.

"Well, what are you waiting for?" I asked coldly. "We leave in twenty minutes."

"Uh, yes sir," he replied meekly, turning on his heels and departing.

The officer returned slowly. He hesitated. "Mr. Davis, will you sign a boarding card?"

"That depends. Let's see it."

He handed one to me. There was a place for nationality, passport number, date and place of issue. And signature.

"Sure," I said, starting to fill it out. For nationality, I inscribed "World Citizen"; for passport number, I wrote: World Service Authority 00001; for date and place of issue, I wrote: "July 4, 1976, Washington, DC." Then I signed.

"Here," I said, handing it back, "all properly filled in."

He took it and read. I glanced at my watch. Fifteen minutes before takeoff. He still stared at the card as if trying to decipher it. If he accepted it, he was accepting the information on it. He, the state of Israel, would then be actually recognizing the WSA passport. On the other hand, if he did not accept it, his choice would be even more difficult: either let me leave without an embarkation card or hold me in Israel against my will.

"I do not think I can accept the information on this card," he said slowly but with little authority in his voice.

"You'd better make up your mind fast," I told him. "I don't think the people here who have suffered so much from official persecution would agree to your detaining me permanently just because I claim the right to identify myself, a stateless person, as a World Citizen. What a mockery your pretensions to democracy and justice would be then."

He stiffened trying to regain his authority but the fight was gone from his eyes.

"All right. You can go" he said without conviction. "But don't ever return to Israel with your world passport."

I smiled and held out my hand. "No hard feelings," I said.

He hesitated, looking at me surprised, then smiling faintly, he took it. His grip was surprisingly firm.

The great plane lifted off the runway and London was only seven hours away. The Holy Land was swiftly fading behind me. But, as my good friend Meyer Levin had suggested to me twenty-eight years earlier, I had, I thought, maybe replanted some "world seeds" in that sacred ground.

****

Appendix

World Government of World Citizens
4002, Basel, Switzerland

Tel Aviv, January 23, 1977

Ephrayin Katzir
President
State of Israel
Jerusalem

Mr. President:

I wish to submit respectfully the following facts relevant to my visit to the Holy Land.

On Friday, January 21st, I left the occupied territory of the State of Israel via the Allenby Bridge after presentation of the Stateless Travel Document, No. 47-704, issued on 31 August, 1973 by the French Prefecture of Mulhouse according to the Convention of 28 September, 1954 of the United Nations.

The Jordanian frontier authorities refused me entry after presentation of my World Service Authority passport, No 018841 issued December 10, 1975 from Basel, Switzerland.

This passport was likewise refused by the Israeli authorities at Ben-Gurion Airport in June, 1976.

The Jordanian military authorities brought me to the center of Allenby Bridge where effectively Jordan's territorial jurisdiction ended. They requested the Israeli military authorities to accept me into Israel on the basis that I had left from there.

I then informed them that I had no further business in Israel and refused to re-enter. I specifically asked the Israeli soldier in charge the law which allowed a forced entry of an individual once he or she had physically left Israel legally. He replied that there was no such law, that Israel was a democratic country.

I remained on the dividing line between Jordan and the occupied territory of Israel, a line which, by definition, cannot be considered as under the territorial jurisdiction of either country.

However, both military authorities of the two states refuted my claim that this dividing line actually existed, therefore I had no legal right to remain on the bridge.

After one-half hour, the Israeli military authorities on instructions from the Israeli government brought me forcibly into Israel and turned me over to the Jericho police.

I was asked for my Stateless Travel Document by the officer in charge. I refused on the basis that my presence in Israel was illegal.

Finally, at the Jerusalem central police station, I was stripped by force and the document taken from me. The exit stamp was subsequently annulled and I was released.

This is to inform you, Mr. President, that I consider myself no longer in the territorial jurisdiction of Israel and that my only document of identity relative to my status is my WSA passport, a World Government document grounded in the Universal Declaration of Human Rights.

Respectfully ,
Garry Davis
World Coordinator

Cc: United Nations, Geneva

37

(Left-right) Mayor Karim Khalif, Toma Sik, myself,
and Mayor Muhamed at the Ramallah City Hall, 1976.

"World territory" on Constantin Quoffa's plot above
Atarot Airport with Toma Sik and Constantin as witnesses.

The Garden of Gethsemanee shot from the police van
transporting me from Jericho to a Jerusalem jail.

A cemetery in Old Jerusalem wherein "Jewish,"
"Moslem" and "Christian" dead are buried side-by-side.

For information about world citizenship and the World Passport:

World Service Authority®
Suite 205
1012 14th Street, NW
Washington, DC 20005

Tel: (202) 638-2662
Fax: (202) 638-0638

Email: info@worldservice.org
Internet: www.worldgovernment.org
www.worldgovernmentfoundation.org

For books and publications:

World Government House
POB 9390
South Burlington, VT 05407

Tel: (802) 864-6818
Fax: (802) 862-3744
Email: worldlaw@globalnetisp.net
Internet: www.worldgovernmenthouse.com

Garry Davis' Web site:
www.garrydavis.org

World Citizen Discussion Forum:
www.groups.yahoo.com/group/WorldCitizen

Endnotes

---

[1] *Webster's New Collegiate Dictionary*, 1960

[2] See Chapter 16, "Who Owns the World?" *World Government, Ready or Not!*, World Government House, 2003

[3] Evening Service

[4] Deuteronomy 6:4

[5] "Lord of the World," Evening Service

[6] "Oh Lord, Give Us Men!" I Maccabees, Ch. 1-4

[7] Literally, "Science of the Absolute"

[8] *My Country is the World*, p. 200, Putnam, 1960

[9] *Washington Post*, Sept. 16, 1979: A story headlined "Israeli forces break up clash of rival Jews." Orthodox Jews, composing a third of Jerusalem's 350,000 residents, were protesting a road passing too close to Orthodox neighborhoods. The road has become a symbol of what Israel's secular majority feels is extremist religious intolerance. The Orthodox Hasidim Jews oppose Zionism even calling for an end to the Jewish state until the "coming of the Messiah."

[10] See "Epilogue to My Country is the World," *World Government, Ready or Not!* (Ibid #2)

[11] Sik v. Attorney-General (1973), (II) 27 P.D. 3 (Registration of nationality)

[12] In Israel, no secular law exists permitting non-religious marriage. Because Toma disclaims being Jewish, he and Bella Sik are therefore "unmarried" in Israeli law.

[13] "One who attacks cherished beliefs as shams." *Webster's New Collegiate Dictionary*, 1960

[14] *Gleanings from the Writings of Baha'u'llah*

[15] *The World Order of Baha'u'llah*, Shoghi Effendi, p. 41

[16] See Chapter 20, "Nationality and Religion," *World Government, Ready or Not!* (Ibid #2)

[17] Ibid, p. 40

[18] Members of the Universal House of Justice are anonymous. I was specifically requested not to reveal the name of my host.

[19] *The World Order of Baha'u'llah*, Shoghi Effendi, p. 36

[20] *The Goal of a New World Order*, Shoghi Effendi, p. 38

[21] See Chapter 6(I) "How World Government Works," *World Government, Ready or Not!* (Ibid #2)

[22] I had laid my world passport on the rock much to the consternation of the Greek Orthodox priest with his smoking brazier which he waved back and forth evidently to "exorcise" any heathen spirits allied with the document!

[23] United Nations Works Relief Association

[24] "Land is the most necessary thing in our establishing roots in Palestine. Since there are hardly any more arable unsettled lands in Palestine, we are bound in each case of purchase of land and its settlement to remove the peasants who cultivated the land thus far, both owners of the land and tenants." Dr. A. Rupin, Jewish Agency expert, in a secret report to the Jewish Agency, 1930. Ref.: Zionist Land-Aggression in Israel, Fouzi el-Asmar

[25] Israel Technological Institute, Haifa (*Haaretz*, April 4, 1969)

[26] "It is a single truth that there is no Zionism, no settlement and no Jewish state without evacuation of Arabs and the expropriation and the fencing of lands." Yeshayahu Ben Porat, *Yediot Aharonot*, (27), July 14, 1972. *Yediot Aharonot* is one of the three largest Hebrew language newspapers in Israel.

[27] On Nov. 9, 1938, 26,000 Jews were sent to concentration camps.

[28] "This card signifies that the bearer whose name and photo appear on the reverse side is a registered citizen of the World Government of World Citizens, founded Sept. 4, 1953 at Ellsworth, Maine, USA. All information inscribed on this card has been notarized or otherwise certified. The World Government of World Citizens is mandated by articles 2, 3, 6, 7, 21(3), 28 and 29 of the Universal Declaration of Human Rights, and by Part 1, art. 1(1), International Covenant on Civil and Political Rights. The bearer is pledged to acknowledge the right and the duty of the World Government of World Citizens to represent him/her in all that concerns the General Good (of humankind) and the Good of All (fundamental human rights). Further, the bearer is committed to assume

sovereign responsibilities and rights on the world civic level whenever and wherever the occasion presents itself. All constituted authority is hereby requested to give all aid and protection to the bearer in the exercise of his/her world citizenship. Violations will be reported to the World Court of Human Rights. By authority of WORLD GOVERNMENT OF WORLD CITIZENS."

[29] Mayor Khalif: "As Palestinian people we are always working for peace and doing a lot for peace not only here in the Middle East but in the whole world. And we all belong of course to the World Government which we are planning to do, all of us…as we belong to our country, Palestine. And we work day and night to have the whole world in one state and to do a lot for its beloved people. As you know, we are Palestinians; we lost everything and we hope that we will come to establish our own state, Palestine, which will be a state in the world state."

Mayor Mulhim: "I fully support the cause of the papers I have just signed because this is what I feel that the human beings all over the world are aspiring to have their human rights given and recognized; to have their daily life and children and families living securely without being threatened by any form of human despondency and tyranny. I felt that the idea should be supported by all the governments and the nations and the individuals of the world as long as it serves the cause of peace and preserving the human rights. And thanks to Mr. Davis who gave me the opportunity and to Mr. Khalif who also gave me the opportunity to be introduced to the group of people carrying the good idea and the best to them all."

[30] See Chapter 16, Who Owns the World? *World Government, Ready or Not!* (Ibid #2)

[31] *My Country is the World*, p. 80. (Ibid #8)

[32] Philip Hodgkins I with his brother John arrived at Plymouth, Mass. on the good ship Mary & John in 1632.

[33] He later changed his name to Ben Davis and was a civil war general.

[34] Jimmy Carter's inauguration

[35] On January 20th, while Constantin, Toma and I were dedicating a tiny piece of land high above Atarot airport to sovereign world law, with only the sun, wind and sky our witnesses, President Jimmy Carter, with one hand on the Holy Bible opened to Micah, Chapter 4, Verse 3, took his Oath of Office. Along with his inaugural address, another message to the "citizens of the world" from the new president of the world's mightiest nation was being transmitted by the Voice of America to the media outside of the United States: "I want to assure you" President Carter informed us world citizens, "that the relations of the United States with other countries and peoples of the world will be guided during our administration by our desire to shape a world order that is more responsive to human aspiration. The United States will meet its obligations to help create a stable, just and peaceful world order. We need your active participation in a joint effort to move the reality of the world closer to the ideals of human freedom and dignity."

[36] 24th Psalm

[37] *Civil Disobedience*, Henry David Thoreau, 1849

[38] Ibid

www.ingramcontent.com/pod-product-compliance
Lightning Source LLC
Chambersburg PA
CBHW081153040426
42445CB00015B/1862